10-3-63

The Brotherhood of Railroad Trainmen

ONE OF A SERIES OF STUDIES OF COMPARATIVE UNION
GOVERNMENTS, EDITED BY WALTER GALENSON FOR THE
CENTER FOR THE STUDY OF DEMOCRATIC INSTITUTIONS

The Brotherhood of

Railroad Trainmen:

The Internal Political Life
of a National Union

Joel Seidman

Professor of Industrial Relations,
University of Chicago

John Wiley and Sons, Inc.

New York and London

Foreword

This is one of a series of monographs on trade union government in the United States commissioned by the Trade Union Study of the Center for the Study of Democratic Institutions, supported by a grant from the Fund for the Republic. The views and judgments that are expressed are those of the author and not necessarily those of the Center or the Fund. Professor Joel Seidman, who was asked to undertake this analysis of the Brotherhood of Railroad Trainmen, has been a prolific writer in the field of industrial relations, and is particularly well known for *The Needle Trades* (1942), *Union Rights and Union Duties* (1943), and *American Labor from Defense to Reconversion* (1953).

The Brotherhood of Railroad Trainmen is the largest of the unions representing the men who operate our trains. It is a stable organization, tracing its origin back to 1883, and its acceptance by employers as part of the industrial relations machinery of the railroads is unquestioned. The only threat to its stability comes from the drastic reduction that is taking place in railroad employment. It faces neither rival labor organizations nor hostile employers.

Professor Seidman finds that the Brotherhood has a strong democratic tradition which greatly tempers the exercise of power by union officials. Factionalism is regarded as a legitimate aspect of the internal political process rather than as a threat to the existence of the organization. National officers, including the president, are regularly opposed for re-election. Moreover, because of the method of electing all national officers one by one rather than from among competing slates, candidates defeated for the top positions usually manage to secure one of the lesser vice-presidencies (there are fifteen of them), and are thus able to maintain a base for future opposition.

Other factors which inhibit the central authority are: the relatively independent intermediate elected officials between the national and local unions; the homogeneity of the membership, their relatively high educational level, and the great degree of job security which they enjoy; and the existence of internal appeals boards not under the direct control of the president. This is not to say that the presidency is an unimportant post. Its incumbent enjoys wide constitutional authority, a great deal of patronage, and all the advantages of publicity through union publications and constant personal contact with members throughout the country. But presidential power has been exercised with restraint for the most part, and where it was not, challenges arose quickly.

An interesting feature of Brotherhood government is the length of conventions, which are held every four years. They normally last for six or seven weeks, and even longer when there are controversial matters. This practice ensures ample time for thorough debate, but it is expensive; the average convention costs $2,500,000. Professor Seidman feels that shorter meetings might save a great deal of money without unduly impairing the union's democracy.

Many other facets of Brotherhood government are analyzed with discernment and objectivity. Professor Seidman has made a significant contribution to our understanding of the requirements of the democratic process not only of trade unions but also of our society more generally.

WALTER GALENSON

Preface

Since the upsurge of unionism in the mass production industries in the 1930's, the railroad brotherhoods have received relatively little attention from academic students of the labor movement. Operating, for the most part, under separate labor legislation in an industry with its peculiar problems and separate
traditions, the railroad brotherhoods have developed their own
distinctive institutional forms and modes of behavior. Yet the
experience of three-quarters of a century or more of successful
operation is one that deserves careful examination, particularly with regard to the internal structure and the balance of
powers that are the focal points of this study. The political
traditions of the Brotherhood of Railroad Trainmen, the largest by far of the operating brotherhoods, offer experience of
value to the American labor movement as a whole.

I am indebted to the Trade Union Study of the Center for
the Study of Democratic Institutions for the opportunity to
participate in this series of monographs and for the financial
support that made the study possible. I wish also to acknowledge
with gratitude the supplementary financial help that I received

from resources at the disposal of the Graduate School of Business of the University of Chicago.

In the course of my investigation I interviewed large numbers of officers, employees, and active members of the Railroad Trainmen, who contributed generously of their time, experience, and insights. Those interviewed were on both sides of the factional conflict that centered about the 1960 convention, and represented quite different, and sometimes contrary, views of the operations of the organization and the behavior of key officials.

I have tried my best to present an objective account of the distribution of authority within the union and the political behavior of its officers and active members. Yet I know that many of those who helped me will be critical of the views expressed at various points in the manuscript. Lest I embarrass any of them by associating their names with the study, I have decided to list none. Nevertheless, I am grateful to them all for the time and effort that they spent in answering my questions and in reading and criticizing the successive drafts of this manuscript.

Some of my academic colleagues have also read the manuscript and given me the benefit of their criticism. I wish to thank Professors Albert Rees, George P. Shultz, Grant McConnell, Arnold R. Weber, and Robert B. McKersie, all of the University of Chicago, and Jacob J. Kaufman of Pennsylvania State University for their suggestions—all of which have improved the manuscript. Finally, I wish to express my thanks to Professor Walter Galenson, editor of this series of monographs, for his cooperation and helpful criticism and advice.

Chicago, Illinois   Joel Seidman
September, 1962

Contents

1

The Railroad Trainmen

Among the operating railroad unions, the Brotherhood of Railroad Trainmen is by far the largest, representing 52 per cent of all railroad operating employees in the United States and Canada. Though its membership is small compared to the giant unions with upwards of a million members found in some other industries, the Brotherhood occupies a secure and respected place in the collective bargaining structure of its industry. At once a protective organization and an insurance society, the Brotherhood services its members on the collective bargaining and grievance front as well as in legislative, political, and fraternal activities. The union is stable in membership and internal structure, orderly in its methods, sound in its finances, persevering in its collective bargaining and grievance work, and conservative in its social philosophy. It enjoys the devoted support of most of the road and yard workers who comprise the bulk of its membership.

The Brotherhood dates its history from 1883, when eight brakemen met in a caboose in the Oneonta, New York, yards of the Delaware and Hudson Railroad to form a benevolent organization. Encouraged by Eugene V. Debs, then a national officer of the Brotherhood of Locomotive Firemen, the Oneonta group launched a national organization of railroad brakemen rather than a local chapter of a nearby railroad benevolent society. Four years later the organization, showing a steady growth in membership, took on protective functions as well, becoming a trade union as well as a benevolent society. Almost from the beginning, the Brotherhood has also been active in legislative work.

As of November 30, 1959, the Brotherhood had more than 1,100 lodges and a total membership of 196,365, of whom 101,825 were non-insurance members. About 21,000 of the total membership were in Canada. Included in the total membership were 36,265 exempted or retired members, who were relieved from the payment of regular dues and assessments. This left a total of approximately 160,000 employed members bearing full financial obligations. The union's bus department, first organized in 1939 and re-established in 1950, had 8,463 members. The Brotherhood had suffered a loss of almost 21,000 members between 1956 and 1959, a reflection of the declining employment on the nation's railroads, after it had reached its all-time membership peak of 217,176 in 1956.[1]

Union Structure

Over the years the union has evolved an internal structure and allocation of powers that is well adapted to the industry in which it operates, and the problems with which it must come to grips. Its basic unit is the subordinate lodge, which is given jurisdiction over workers in one or more seniority districts in road, yard, or bus service. While the subordinate lodge functions as a unit for general administrative purposes, its most important business, the handling of time claims and other grievances, is a function of that portion of its membership with seniority rights in the yard, road, or bus division in which the grievance arises. Each such seniority district has its own local grievance committee headed by a local chairman, an officer who, except for ceremonial purposes, is far more important than the lodge president. The local chairmen of the lodges on a single railroad or bus company—or, in the case of some very large roads, a major administrative unit thereof—comprise the general committee that is in charge of the collective bargaining and grievance work on that line. The chairman of a general committee is the most important union functionary on the road, except when, at his request, an officer of the Grand Lodge is sent on the property to assist him. The general chairmen, in turn, are organized into the International Association of General Chairmen, which serves as an advisory body to the national president of the Brotherhood on national collective bargaining issues.

A parallel structure exists to promote the legislative objectives of the union. To a far greater extent than most other unions, the railroad brotherhoods have a choice between collective bargaining and legislative means to achieve an objective, because of the long tradition of government regulation of the railroads and the close relationship of railroad equipment and operating rules to the safety of the traveling public. The hazardous nature of railroad employment early turned the attention of the Brotherhood, along with that of the other operating unions, to the legislative process, particularly when the unions were too weak, in an economic sense, to compel the carriers to adopt the best safety devices available. If desired hours or minimum crews on trains, similarly, could not be obtained at the collective bargaining table, the legislative process, at both the federal and the state levels, might be available for their achievement. Much the same situation exists in Canada, except that in the Dominion, the federal government, not the provinces, has jurisdiction over legislation affecting the railroads.

In both the United States and Canada, the Brotherhood tends to use legislative pressure to supplement its collective bargaining efforts. Yet whether the railroad unions are relatively stronger on the economic or the political front depends in large part on current economic conditions, as well as on the political climate of the moment. When the Republicans are in power in Washington or when southern Democrats hold the key Congressional posts, the unions may do better in collective bargaining, provided economic conditions are favorable. When northern Democrats hold the reins of power, on the other hand, gains are more likely to be achieved through legislative influence rather than through the use of economic strength. Similar considerations affect the efforts to obtain state legislation. Federal or state legislation, once enacted, must be policed; and the Brotherhood, like the other rail unions, assembles complaints of violations from its members and brings them to the attention of the responsible authorities.

Each lodge elects a legislative representative to represent it in this area of activity; the legislative representatives in a state comprise the state legislative board, which is headed by the state legislative representative. Their work, in turn, is coordinated through the National Conference of State Legislative Representatives. The interests of the Brotherhood in federal legislation are looked after by the national legislative representative. In Canada a comparable structure exists, with legislative representatives in the provinces, in addition to a Canadian legislative representative who is stationed in Ottawa.

In its benevolent functions the organization operates through the Brotherhood of Railroad Trainmen Insurance Department, which is separately incorporated, and through which union members or members of their families may purchase death, disability, endowment, accident and health, or other types of insurance policies. Any qualified member may carry up to $5,000.00 of insurance with total and permanent disability benefits, plus an additional $5,000.00 without such benefits. The insurance remains in effect only so long as the member maintains his good standing in the Brotherhood. When he leaves the union, his insurance equity is paid to him in cash and his certificates become void (except if he is expelled under charges, he may continue in the Insurance Department if he so desires). The member who elects not to purchase an insurance policy suffers a political disability, in that he becomes ineligible to be a delegate to the union's conventions, which legislate on insurance as well as on other matters. The member who wishes to play an active role in the Trainmen at the international union level must, therefore, become an insurance member of the union.

There is general agreement that while the union's protective function is vastly more important than the insurance feature in recruiting members, the insurance helps to keep men in the Brotherhood, particularly after middle age has been reached. Young men, in view of the hazardous nature of the occupation, tend to be more interested in accident than in life policies. Those who do not take out insurance of any type, the union has found over the years, are less likely to keep up their membership. Brotherhood insurance is to be preferred to comparable policies from commercial companies, since the policies are easier to obtain, the costs are more moderate, and the union is more liberal in the payment of benefits. The insurance had been much cheaper until 1931, when the union, finding that its insurance funds were in a precarious position, changed from an assessment to a reserve basis, simultaneously increasing its charges by a substantial amount.

Each lodge has one or more insurance representatives, usually including the treasurer, who counsel members on their insurance needs. The activities of the insurance representatives, in turn, are directed by full-time officers called field supervisors, who are paid on a commission basis like insurance agents representing commercial companies, and who also have responsibilities for bringing members into the union. The field supervisors are appointed by the president and function as part of the Promotion Department of the Grand Lodge.

All these various activities of the Brotherhood are supervised by the Grand Lodge, which consists of a number of national officers headed by the president, a series of administrative boards, and a delegate from each subordinate lodge. At periodic intervals, now normally every fourth year, the delegates assemble in convention as the Grand Lodge. The Trainmen have a powerful president, who exercises supervision over the other national officers and over subordinate lodges. The union's vice presidents are in a dependent position, subject to the president for allocation of territory and assignments of work. The general secretary and treasurer is in a somewhat more independent position, since his area of responsibility is determined by constitutional provision. A large number of boards—a Board of Directors, a Board of Trustees and Insurance, a Board of Appeals, and an Executive Board—help to keep power diffused, as contrasted with the more typical national union situation in which a single general executive board performs a variety of functions.

Despite its strong presidency, the Brotherhood has always enjoyed a vigorous internal life. Throughout its history there have been spirited contests for office, at the international as well as at the local level. In contrast with the situation found in many international unions, in which a president who seeks re-election is rarely challenged, in the Brotherhood it is unusual for a convention to re-elect the incumbent without contest. Of the fifteen conventions held between 1909 and 1960, the presidency was contested at eleven. In most of these contests, personalities, rather than different views of union functions or philosophy, have been the primary issues—though in some cases the two have tended to coalesce, as when a more vigorous or militant candidate has challenged one who was more conservative in his social philosophy or more conciliatory in his approach to the carriers.

In addition to posts controlled by the national officers, a number of full-time union positions, satisfying in both an economic and a psychological sense, are available within the union's structure, affording ambitious members an opportunity to learn leadership skills, acquire valuable experience, and build a secure and independent political base. Conventions that last five to seven weeks, while a source of great expense, give the delegates ample opportunity to know each other and to become acquainted with issues and candidates. A Trainmen's convention, consequently, is not one that is easily manipulated by a national head. All of these factors, plus the absence of a union security clause until recently, and the unusual type that now exists for railroad transportation workers, help to explain the democratic tendencies that prevail in the union.

Roadmen and Yardmen

The Brotherhood of Railroad Trainmen is composed of two main groups of workers, roadmen and yardmen, who work as switchmen, brakemen, or conductors. Workers falling within the Trainmen's jurisdiction include the conductor of a road or yard crew—also called yard foreman in the latter case—who is in charge of the crew's operations; the head brakeman of a road crew, who may serve as ticket collector on a passenger train; the rear brakeman or flagman, and also the baggageman, of a road crew; and the switchmen, also called yard helpers, of a yard crew. Other miscellaneous groups of railroad workers, such as switchtenders, car retarder operators, and yardmasters, are also eligible for membership, as are drivers and other employees of bus lines. Until the rapid and recent decline in the volume of railroad employment set in, causing the furloughing of workers with up to ten or fifteen or more years of seniority on many lines, the members of the

Brotherhood, protected by a strong union and by strict seniority rules, enjoyed a high degree of job security in a vital industry.

The membership is homogeneous in terms of educational background and reasonably so with regard to skill and level of pay. Prior to World War I all that was required in the way of educational background was an ability to read and write, for which a fourth-grade education might suffice. Many of the present leaders of the union entered the industry when an eighth-grade education was required, and more recently the railroads have been insisting on high school graduation whenever the state of the labor market permitted. The more desirable working assignments, in terms of hours and opportunities for overtime work, go to the top seniority men, positions which all workers in their turn may achieve. Average annual earnings for brakemen for the year 1957 ranged from $5,455.00 to $7,006.00, and for conductors from $6,921.00 to $8,440.00, depending on whether they were employed in through freight, passenger, or local freight service.[2] High seniority conductors on through trains may now earn up to $12,000.00, depending on the mileage run and the opportunities for overtime. Yard workers usually earn less than road workers, since they are paid on a time basis instead of the dual time or miles system, and since they cannot profit from the high speed of modern trains. Annual earnings in Canada average from 10 to 20 per cent less than the corresponding classes of workers earn in the United States.

The line of progression is from brakeman or switchman to conductor. Typically in road service, a brakeman, after three years or 72,000 miles, must take an examination in operating rules, train orders, and the like, to qualify as a conductor. If he fails the first examination, he is tested again ninety days later, and dropped from the service if he fails a second time. When his turn comes according to the seniority list he must then move up to a conductor's position, unless there is an agreement on the road that a man may waive his seniority and remain a brakeman permanently.

The yardmen, working closely together on regular shifts and seeing the other shifts as they relieve each other, develop strong group feelings. They also see switching crews of other railroads in the same city as they interchange cars. Information passes quickly from crew to crew, and from road to road within a metropolitan switching district. Those in large terminals are in a strong strategic position in relation to management, since much of the freight traffic of the nation must travel through a few major switching yards and terminals. Working in larger cities, moreover, they are in a position to know of alternative types of employment that may be available, though their mobility is limited by the fact that their skill is not transferable. Roadmen, by way of contrast, are relatively isolated on the job, though they have ample opportunities for conversation while in the yards. Small town switchmen are likely to be the most isolated group among the Trainmen. Big city switchmen, as a result of all these factors, are likely to be the most independent in relation to management and to show the greatest militancy and solidarity. For much the same reasons, switchmen in the major metropolitan centers are likely to be in the forefront of any movement of political insurgency within the union.

The feeling of solidarity among switchmen and brakemen is heightened by their relative homogeneity, as contrasted with workers in industrial unions, in terms of education, skill, or pay. After passing a fairly rigid physical examination, an applicant goes through a training program that may last for three days or more, during which time he becomes acquainted with railroad signals, safety requirements, working rules, and company regulations. He then takes his place on the extra list, subject to call, and earning the standard rate as he works, the rest of his learning taking place on the job. As his seniority mounts he works more regularly, and after a time he is protected by his place on the seniority roster against minor fluctuations in business. After a few years he is promoted to conductor, in accordance with seniority and the requirements of the railroad.

The job attracts men who prefer outdoor work, and who value the relative freedom and mobility of the switchman's job. Once the conductor in charge of a switching crew receives his instructions, his crew is pretty much on its own, doing the work in the light of their experience, roaming with their engine over the yard as switching requirements dictate, and going on the property of other railroads to interchange cars. They do not punch a time clock; instead, the conductor, the foreman of the crew, fills out the time sheets. The work is more regular than in most types of industrial employment, and there are opportunities for over-time as the particular job may require.

On the other hand, the job has its share of disadvantages. Since the railroad is in continuous operation, many must work nights, Sundays, and holidays, at the cost of disrupting normal family life. Despite substantial safety improvements in recent decades, the switchman's job remains the most dangerous on the railroad, and in addition he must work outdoors regardless of the weather, in heat or cold, rain or snow. Though overtime pay is almost al-ways welcomed, the individual worker has no choice as to whether or when he shall work beyond his normal quitting time; he and the rest of his crew are simply required to finish the work as-signed to them. In recent years relatively little railroad employ-ment has been available to new workers, and these jobs have not been very attractive because of the danger of lay-offs to low sen-iority workers in a period of declining employment.

Whereas during the depression period of the 1930's railroad employment was preferable to working in a factory (both with regards to pay and regularity of employment), much of the rela-tive pay advantage has since been lost. Also seniority systems in factories now typically give protection to the workers against lay-offs out of turn. The man who can work his way into a fairly highly skilled factory job, moreover, may enjoy higher earnings than a switchman, on a yearly as well as on an hourly basis. As a result the switchman's job lost in relative appeal, and the turn-over rate climbed noticeably as depressed conditions gave way to relatively full employment. Brakemen generally agree that the status of their job has declined in recent years, particularly in metropolitan areas.[3]

Since yardmen and roadmen are employed throughout the country, they tend to be representative of the entire population, from rural areas and small towns to the major metropolitan cen-ters. Railroad men agree, however, that the jobs are relatively more desirable to young men growing up in small towns, who may have fewer attractive types of employment available to them. There is a noticeable tendency for sons to follow their fathers into railroading, a tendency heightened by the relative lack of other industries at many railroad division points. In terms of religion and ethnic origin, brakemen probably represent a cross section of the population, except that Negroes have generally been barred from this type of work, and the most recent immigrant groups, lacking the necessary language and educational requirements, seldom have been able to qualify.

Internal Divisions and Minority Groups

The distinction between yard and road work, where separate seniority rosters are maintained for each and penalty payments are prescribed if work boundaries are overstepped, can create a political division within the union. While the two groups unite to press for gains benefiting both, whether through collective bargaining negotiations or legislation, they both know that the volume of employment for brakemen would diminish if the carriers were permitted to assign men to types of work, interchangeably and without penalty, now classified as either road or yard. In most terminal and division points the road and yard rosters are now combined under what is known as "top and bottom" seniority, a plan under which each group of workers is added to the bottom of the other's seniority list.

Recent political divisions within the union have not depended on the distinction between road and yard work, although there have been suggestions that in some contests in the past the two groups of men have tended to line up on opposite sides. When there is a difference over the tactics to be employed against the railroads, the tendency, for reasons already suggested, is for yard lodges in metropolitan centers to take the more aggressive position. There is also some feeling on their part that the allocation of voting strength at Trainmen conventions, one delegate with one vote to a lodge regardless of its size, discriminates against them, since roadmen, strung out along the length and breadth of the railroad system, tend to have a larger number of lodges in proportion to their membership.

In a number of cases, groups of yard and road workers have combined to form a single lodge, showing that feelings of solidarity outweigh any differences of interest between them. Should these differences become acute, they could quickly be translated into rival political groupings within the lodge. A similar situation exists where men employed by two or more railroads combine into a single lodge. In either case, if a group felt that its interests were being ignored because another seniority district controlled the lodge, it could seek approval to form a separate lodge of its own.

Another internal difference is based on age, as might be expected in an industry in which the rights of workers in relationship to each other are governed so largely by seniority. The belief that seniority should govern the choice of runs as well as layoffs is deeply ingrained in the thinking of road workers; and the younger men, if only their health remains good and they stay in the same seniority district, may look forward to having some day their share of the fast runs, which produce high earnings under the dual system of pay by time or miles. But differences arise with regard to the amount of mileage that senior men may accumulate in a single month. While the figure may vary from road to road, often the mileage is limited to 4,500, thus providing more desirable work opportunities to the younger men during the last few days of the monthly work period. The younger men would like to see the maximum monthly mileage reduced, but they are handicapped by the influence of older men in the lodges and in negotiations with management. The steady decline in the volume of railroad employment tends to intensify the control of the older men. No comparable problem arises in yard work, where the standard five-day work week is in effect; while seniority is also important there, governing the choice of work assignments and the order of lay-off and recall to work, it carries no comparable disparity in earnings and hours—although yard jobs that tend to work overtime regularly are certain to be obtained by men high on the seniority list. The age difference is also reflected in the movement for compulsory retirement, from union office as well as from service on the railroads.

No other internal difference is a factor in the life of the union today. In the past, sectional differences at times have been of some consequence; during the first quarter of this century, there was a persistent and often bitter rivalry between the East and the West which, on one or two occasions, according to an historian of the union, threatened to break up the organization.[4] There is also a belief on the part of workers in larger cities that their pay should be higher than that of small town residents, though this difference in interest has never been translated into political pressures within the organization.

Discrimination against Negroes has been practiced both by the carriers and by the union. Railroads usually have not hired Negroes as brakemen when a sufficient number of white applicants were available. The Brotherhood, for its part, from its formation and for approximately the first three-quarters of a century of its existence, limited membership by constitutional provision to white males. Beginning in 1945, however, a number of states passed laws prohibiting discrimination in employment because of race, and outlawing similar discrimination by unions as to rights and privileges of membership. In 1954 the Trainmen amended their constitution, not to remove the restriction of membership to whites, but to provide that the clause would not apply where it was in conflict with state law.

In 1957 the Trainmen affiliated with the AFL-CIO, after remaining independent for virtually three-quarters of a century. The Firemen, which also discriminated against Negroes, joined the Federation at the same time. Before its merger with the CIO in December, 1955, the AFL had not insisted that its affiliated national unions admit Negroes to membership on equal terms, on the ground that each such affiliate was autonomous. The constitution of the merged body, however, called for full union benefits for all workers regardless of race, creed, color, or national origin, and established a Committee on Civil Rights to work toward the elimination of racial discrimination within the labor movement.

As a condition of their affiliation with the Federation, as a result, both the Trainmen and the Firemen pledged to eliminate their Negro exclusion clauses at their next conventions, and the Trainmen took this action when they next met in convention early in 1960. In the meantime, however, they had admitted a substantial number of Negroes, even in states that did not have legislation barring discrimination by unions. In a number of places the railroads had hired Negroes as switchmen, simply because, in the tight labor market during and following World War II, it was hard to get a sufficiently large number of qualified white applicants. Where this happened the local lodges generally admitted the Negroes to membership, since otherwise they would have lost control, to that extent, over their jurisdiction. In some cases white workers were unhappy about the hiring of Negroes, not so much because of racial prejudice as because they would lose welcome overtime work as a result. A number of Negroes are also employed in the bus industry, particularly on the West coast, where several hundred are members of a single bus lodge affiliated with the Brotherhood. Interestingly enough, one Negro delegate was in attendance at the convention that removed the bar against Negro membership. The Negro membership of the Brotherhood now fluctuates between 1,500 and 3,000.

Under a resolution adopted by the 1954 convention, membership in the union was denied to communists or to believers in any form of tyranny seeking to overthrow democracy or change its institutions by violent means.[5] Under this resolution, charges were preferred in 1958 against a member for affiliation with the Communist Party, the charges being sustained by a trial committee. The lodge, after accepting the trial committee's findings, voted 16 to expel and 10 to reprimand, the necessary two-thirds vote for expulsion failing by a narrow margin. The member who had preferred the charges appealed to President W. P. Kennedy, who set aside the order of reprimand and ordered the lodge to expel the accused member. He, in turn, appealed the lodge's expulsion action, but his appeal was denied by the Board of Directors.[6]

Women are barred constitutionally from membership in the union, the provision defining qualifications for membership limiting applicants to males. This is not a reflection of male exclusiveness nor a desire to avoid the competition of women in the labor market, but a reflection of the fact that only men are now hired for the dangerous jobs as switchmen or brakemen at which virtually all railroaders under the union's jurisdiction start their working careers. When women occasionally are employed within the union's jurisdiction, at such jobs as hostesses on passenger trains or buses (or, as during World War II, at brakemen's jobs) they are accepted into the union.

Representation Elections and Collective Bargaining

Jurisdictional rivalries among the various craft unions operating on the railroads have kept the National Mediation Board busy with elections and absorbed much of the funds and energies of the unions. The Conductors and the Trainmen overlap almost completely in road, though not in yard, service; and yard foremen, helpers, and switchtenders may join the unions of the Trainmen, the Switchmen or in unusual cases even the Conductors. Each union seeks to expand its membership at the expense of its rivals, finding supporters among employees in the unit who are dissatisfied with the internal politics of the bargaining agency or with the representation they have received in disputes with the carriers. Some of the unions, when they lose bargaining rights on a property, maintain skeletal lodges until it is timely to raise the question again. Representation elections on the railroads have typically ceased to be issues between union and management; instead they are contests between rival unions, incessantly seeking to raid or to protect themselves against raids. A proposed merger of the Trainmen and Conductors holds promise of ending a large and important category of jurisdictional squabbles.

Collective bargaining on the railroads[7] is a mixture of national bargaining, in which the Grand Lodge takes the leadership, and bargaining over local issues on the individual railroads. Although certification under the Railway Labor Act as amended is for a craft or class of employees on a single railroad, the practice of bargaining on this basis has steadily diminished in importance. Regional bargaining was begun by the operating crafts in 1902; there were national agreements in the World War I period of government administration, and national bargaining, or something very close to it, has been engaged in on a craft or joint craft basis since 1931.

National bargaining on wages has readily accommodated itself to the legal requirements of collective bargaining with the union representing a majority of a craft or class on an individual road. When a national wage movement gets under way, the thirty-day notices required under the Railway Labor Act are served separately for each established bargaining unit. The changes that are requested are identical, however, and each notice contains a request that, should the dispute not be settled between the union and the carrier, it be referred to the national committees set up to represent both sides. Once this is done, the real bargaining gets under way with the heads of the cooperating unions on one side of the bargaining table and representatives of the three regional associations of carriers on the other.

National bargaining does not mean that the views of local

lodge officers and members are unimportant or ignored. Local groups and individual officers or members are likely to bombard the national office with their opinions at critical points in the negotiations, such as when an emergency board appointed under the terms of the Railway Labor Act, as amended, submits its report and recommendations. In his account of the 1949-1951 rules-wage movement, for example, President Kennedy of the Trainmen asserted that "No sooner had the Board's report hit the nation's press and *Trainman News* than thousands of wires, letters and postcards poured into my office protesting the recommendations with all the vitriolic terms at disposal of the senders." [8] Though a national officer on occasion may seek to stimulate such a flow of communications in order to bolster his position in dealing with the carriers or with the government, it is, nevertheless, true that elected officers in an organization such as the Trainmen, where contests for national office are the rule rather than the exception, cannot afford to disregard the sentiments of their members in matters as vital as a national rules-wage movement.

The development of national collective bargaining in the past thirty years has not resulted in the atrophy of collective bargaining at the level of the individual carrier, since many issues remain to be worked out at that level between management and the general committees representing the various crafts among the employees. Among the important issues which are now handled separately on each road are mileage limitations and the question of compulsory retirement. Many of the problems, indeed, such as the places of starting and stopping work, have to be worked out separately at each terminal. In general it may be said that issues that would have an important impact on the competitive situation of one railroad in relation to another are now handled through national bargaining, whereas matters that involve local preference or convenience are settled separately on each road, even though such local decisions may also affect costs. This arrangement gives the general committees and the subordinate lodges important work to do, and helps to keep the organization vitalized despite the flow of power over wage rates and important rules to the national officers. Despite the rise of national bargaining, negotiations are still carried on separately by some roads, and on all there is ample scope for local bargaining to settle particular local problems. Much the same situation exists in Canada with regard to national wage-rules movements on the one hand and bargaining on the individual properties on the other.

Another aspect of railroad collective bargaining that has an impact on the rights and the behavior of Brotherhood members is the union security provision, which differs from the conventional types found in other industries. Under the 1934 amendments to the Railway Labor Act, the union shop, along with other forms of union security, was outlawed; at that time the railroad unions were still combating the menace of the company union, and accepted the ban on the union shop and the checkoff as part of the section that outlawed management assistance to a labor organization. The Trainmen accepted this ban on union security arrangements somewhat reluctantly, since the effect was to render illegal the "percentage agreements" that the union had negotiated with a number of roads, under which the carriers had agreed that a specified percentage of the workers would be members of the Brotherhood. The number of non-unionists has since been kept down, however, by group pressure against "no-bills"—a term for freight for which there are no way bills, and therefore no known destination, and applied by unionists to those who refused to join—and by the desire of men for union representation should they have a grievance against their employer. Whereas workers in other industries, under similar circumstances, might simply be concerned with pay rates and protection from company disciplinary measures, on the railroads the technical rules on seniority, craft jurisdictional lines, and wage payments create a large number of pay claims, which a worker could hardly hope to handle by himself.

In 1951, after the company unions had long since disappeared, the railroad unions persuaded Congress to amend the Railway Labor Act to legalize the union shop and the check-off. Some workers had a record of dropping union membership when things were going well, rejoining whenever they had a grievance; others dropped out if they became disgruntled, as when an insurance claim that they submitted was not allowed. The railroad operating unions had a special problem with the union shop, however, because a man might work within a single pay period both as a brakeman and as a conductor, or as a fireman as well as an engineer. It seemed unreasonable to require him to join two organizations, and no organization wanted to lose members who preferred it to its rivals. Accordingly, the provision was written, with respect to engine, train, and yard service, to require union membership, not necessarily in the union with bargaining rights, but in any union that was national in scope and admitted members of the particular craft or class. Employees were also allowed to change from one organization to another, despite the negotiation of a union shop clause. Some workers—"double-headers," they are called—prefer to keep up membership in two unions, for the sake of insurance features, friendship patterns, prestige factors, or other reasons.

Where the Brotherhood has a union shop clause in effect, therefore, a worker may hold his job by belonging to the unions of the Conductors or the Switchmen, if for any reasons he finds the Trainmen's organization not to his liking. This gives the member a certain independence in relation to the union, and forces the officers to be more responsive to the desires of the membership and more considerate of their feelings than they otherwise might be. The option of joining one of the rival bodies, however, is available only where there is a lodge in the same area that a worker may join. If the lodge is too far distant it would be unable to give him representation in dealings with management, though a dues receipt from it would probably protect him from discharge if the lodge holding the contract sought his dismissal under the union shop provision. If the proposed merger of the Trainmen and the Conductors is effected, the union shop, so far as workers within the Trainmen's jurisdiction is concerned, will more nearly approach that found in other industries, except for yardmen in areas in which the Switchmen's Union has lodges.

In Canada, as in the United States, union security provisions on the railroads are of relatively recent origin. As in the United States, most railroad workers joined the union of their craft, though a small number refused for a variety of reasons—because they wished to save dues, because they disliked the lodge officers, or because they wanted to belong to a purely Canadian organization. In recent years preference of employment has become the most usual type of union security among the railroad operating groups in Canada. Under this arrangement, the man who does not pay union dues goes to the bottom of the spare board, though he can keep his place on the seniority list by paying merely the union's protective assessment, avoiding the share of dues that goes to support legislative work or the activities of the Grand Lodge.

Because many of the railroad unions in the United States discriminated against Negroes, the 1951 amendments to the Railway Labor Act provided that the requirement to join a union did not apply to workers to whom membership was not available on the same terms and conditions applicable to others. Neither did it apply to those whose membership was denied or terminated for any reason other than the failure to tender dues, initiation fees, or assessments. Since 1951, as a result of these amendments, the union shop has been spreading on the railroads, though the provisions referred to above make its operation among the railroad operating workers somewhat different from the rest of American industry.

Jobs, Work Rules, and Mergers

The current plight in which the railroads find themselves has contributed to dissatisfaction within the ranks of the Brotherhood. Whereas most American industry has expanded in the past quarter of a century, with profit margins ample much of the time, the railroads, except for the wartime demand for their services, have been in a long period of decline. Railroad workers, once part of this country's aristocracy of labor, have enjoyed a somewhat less rapid advance in weekly wages since the late 1930's than manufacturing workers have received,[9] as the economic plight of their industry tempered their gains. Meanwhile the rise of competing transportation facilities, combined with technological advance and a strong impulse toward merger of competing facilities and abandonment of branch lines, have reduced railroad employment from 1,400,000 in 1945 to approximately 800,000 in 1961.

Railroad management has sought in part to meet its problems by a spirited public attack upon outmoded rules and alleged "featherbedding" [10] in the industry, pointing particularly to the length of the day's run,[11] the separation of road and yard work, the size or "consist" of a crew, and the issue of the fireman on diesel locomotives. The first three of these issues bear directly upon the number of workers in the Brotherhood's jurisdiction that the industry will need. As a result of the carriers' pressure, a Presidential Railroad Commission was appointed late in 1960 to investigate the work rules issue. The threat of a further decline in railroad employment, particularly among the operating crafts, created widespread apprehension among railroad workers, and made the task of union leadership particularly difficult. While the heads of unions in expanding industries were making economic gains, the leaders of railroad unions were largely on the defensive, appearing in the public eye as defenders of rules denounced as uneconomic and outmoded by railroad management.

Beyond question, this is one of the most critical periods in the history of railroad unionism. The economic plight of the carriers, the sharp decline in the number of workers employed, the investigation by a federal commission of work rules valued highly by the workers, and the accelerated movement toward mergers have combined to put the labor organizations under serious strain and their officers on the defensive. Periods such as this tend to produce rival leaders who find the membership, disturbed and anxious, in a mood to listen to their criticism of the administration and its policies. There is no more opportune moment than now for a study of the structure of authority within the union, of the duties and powers of the officers, and of the forces that make for control from the top or for an effectively functioning democracy.

2

The Subordinate Lodge

The subordinate lodge occupies a vital place in the structure of the Brotherhood. It is here that the member belongs, it is here that he takes his questions and his grievances relating to his work situation, and it is here that he has an opportunity to discuss and register his opinion on the many aspects of Brotherhood affairs. The vitality of the entire organization depends to no small degree upon the effective conduct of business at the local lodge level.

Since the membership of the Brotherhood is spread out across the United States and Canada wherever railroads operate, the organization of the men into lodges for the transaction of their business presents some difficulties. For purposes of bargaining, the union must follow the lines of seniority districts as established by the railroads, though often these districts contain too few men to meet the financial burden that creation of a separate lodge entails, and in other cases they start work, and therefore are likely to live, at points so far distant that meetings are attended with great difficulty. Yards that are fifty or even one hundred or more miles apart may be serviced from a single seniority list, in which case the high seniority men are likely to choose assignments in the same yard regularly, and make their homes nearby—though low seniority men may have to take assignments in either place; wherever the lodge is established, the location is bound to be inconvenient for one group of men. Once a satisfactory lodge structure is set up, moreover, a decline in employment, a reorganization of working schedules, the elimination of a division point, the establishment of a new yard or the elimination of an old one, a consolidation of facilities, or a merger of formerly independent railroads may make it advisable to consolidate existing lodges, form new ones, or reassign some portion of the membership.

A subordinate lodge, which must have at least ten members, comes into existence by virtue of a charter granted by the president of the Brotherhood, with the jurisdiction assigned to it by the president. The lodge consists of the men in one or more road or yard seniority districts, on one or more railroads. Bus men may either be in a separate lodge or in one with groups of railroaders. While the number of seniority districts in a single lodge is usually between one and five, occasionally the number may run as high as eight, nine, or even ten. The number depends upon such considerations as economy of operation, convenience of location, and desires of the groups involved. A typical lodge may have from 100 to 300 members, though the number may vary from under 50 to over 1,000.

When the organization of a new lodge is proposed in a place where one or more lodges already exist, the consent of the nearest lodge is obtained before the new charter may be issued; if such consent is refused, an appeal may be made to the president of the Brotherhood, whose decision is final. The president also has authority to authorize (upon request) the removal of a lodge from one town to another, to merge lodges in the same locality, and to revoke the charter of a lodge for proper cause after investigation and hearing. A charter may be revoked for improper conduct, for failure to conform to the union's constitution and regulations, for neglecting to hold at least one regular meeting each month, or for other reasons specified in the constitution.

From time to time there are clashes of interest between lodges growing out of the jurisdiction assigned them. Thus a lodge may object when jurisdiction over a group of workers at a particular point is taken from it and assigned to a neighboring lodge, or when exclusive jurisdiction over an area is changed to joint jurisdiction with another lodge. In disputes of this sort the president is likely to follow the recommendations made by the general committee on the property, though if the case is a particularly difficult one he may send a Grand Lodge officer to the scene to investigate the problem and recommend a solution. Where a carrier consolidates service involving two seniority districts represented by separate lodges, it usually gives each group of men prior rights to the work it always performed, though a question may arise with regard to jurisdiction over men hired after the date of consolidation. Although merger of the lodges might be a logical solution, one lodge—presumably the one that would be in the minority should merger occur—might object strenuously to such a course of action.[1] Nor can the president always impose such a solution, especially where the men feel strongly enough about the issue to leave the Brotherhood for a rival organization, should they fail to get a settlement satisfactory to them.

The reverse of this situation also occurs, as where a lodge is made up of employees of several carriers who hold their seniority at different points. At whatever place the lodge meets, the location is bound to be convenient to some portion of the membership and inconvenient to others. Under such circumstances, at the request of a substantial number of the members, the president may create an additional lodge, giving it jurisdiction over the seniority district or districts whose workers found the meetings difficult to attend. To set up this lodge, the president would consider the desires of the men, the distance that they would have to travel, and the additional financial burden that creation of a new lodge would entail.[2]

Sometimes a group of workers may feel that their interests are insufficiently looked after, not because of the location or jurisdiction of their lodge, but because they lack their own local chairman with an interest in their problems. Where road and yard workers on a carrier have the same local chairman, the smaller group may be outvoted in the election of a local chairman, and dissatisfied with the service it receives from him. If there is disagreement as to whether election of a separate local chairman for the smaller group is to be permitted, the issue goes to the general committee on the railroad for decision. Here the decision may be favorable, to allow the group the desired representation, or unfavorable, because of the size of the general committee and the increased expense that would result. [3] Still another type of situation arises where a carrier acquires a subsidiary whose employees, though now covered by the same agreement, are on a separate seniority roster. Where the two groups of men work in a single terminal area, they may be represented by the same local chairman; however, if the minority group is dissatisfied with his handling of their cases they would likely seek a local chairman of their own. Switchtenders, similarly, may be on a separate seniority roster from yardmen, but be represented by a yardmen's committee which lacks familiarity with the rules and agreements governing the work of switchtenders. Whereas in such a situation the switchtenders may request a separate lodge, the better solution may be to allow them to elect their own local committee, so that they will have a local chairman from their own ranks to process their claims and grievances.[4]

If two groups of men are to be represented successfully by the same local committee, the majority must usually be willing to permit members of the minority to be elected to some of the positions. The majority group, understandably enough, is likely to elect the local chairman from its ranks, reserving either the vice chairmanship or the secretary's post for the other group. Where a seniority district of yardmen covers two yards, similarly, the vice chairman or the secretary typically will be chosen from the yard that does not furnish the local chairman. A lodge that includes two or more seniority districts, each with its own local chairman, limits the vote on matters affecting one of the districts to the workers holding seniority there, though all members of the lodge may discuss the issue.

Lodge Meetings, Officers, and Finances

Brotherhood officers, like those of almost every other union, echo the complaint that lodge meetings are poorly attended. The average lodge, with a membership of perhaps 150, is fortunate to get more than a dozen or so members to its regular meetings, usually held monthly, or, in some cases, twice monthly. A lodge of 100, visited by the author, had 15 in attendance at its regular meeting, the best attendance in percentage terms that he happened to find. One of 200 members had 17 present, and two lodges of 300 each had, respectively, only 7 and 8. Another lodge of almost 500 had 20 at one meeting, but turned out 55 at another after the men had been notified that an action affecting their seniority—and therefore their opportunity to earn—would be on the agenda. A critical issue, such as a threatened strike, will bring a third to a half of the members, or even more, to a meeting. Attendance of railroad workers at union meetings presents difficulties not found in many other industries, since the railroads are in continuous operation and since road workers may be spread out over a hundred miles or more along the territory covered by the district.

If these meetings were at all representative of the manner in which the 1,100 lodges of the Brotherhood conduct their business, the organization beyond question is democratic at the grass roots. Ample opportunity was given each member to introduce motions, discuss items of business before the body, or express his views or his complaints about his work problems and the conduct of Brotherhood affairs. In some instances, indeed, the presiding officer was too permissive, allowing members to speak without being recognized, to make personal attacks on officers they disliked, and to wander in their remarks from the topic under discussion, so that it was sometimes difficult to conduct business in an orderly fashion.

Members showed by their questions and comments that they considered themselves the employers, not the servants, of their paid officers—particularly of their local chairman and their general chairman. If they were dissatisfied with their local chairman they raised the question of his pay, and suggested that it might be too high in view of the service they were getting; they asked when the local chairman had last been at their place of work and on their shift; they criticized their general chairman, where they felt he was not pushing their grievances with sufficient vigor, and occasionally authorized a letter that bluntly invited—almost ordered—him to attend the next meeting of their lodge. Members were apt to hold the local chairman responsible for any deterioration of conditions; whereas the local chairmen, in turn, were apt to criticize the men for allowing management officials to violate the rules of their agreement without reporting the facts promptly to their officers so that protests could be made or time claims filed.

Occasionally some embarrassment is caused by the presence in the lodge meeting of a member who is a management official. A Brotherhood member promoted into management ranks may keep up his union membership if he wishes, and many do so for the sake of the insurance policies the union offers, or for protection in the event they are ever demoted to the ranks of non-supervisory employees. To prevent conflict-of-interest situations from arising, the Brotherhood often does not collect the grievance assessment from management officials, nor does it permit them a vote on grievance matters, though these practices vary among units of the Trainmen. There are times, however, when the very presence of management personnel may have an inhibiting effect on the discussion, as where the official whose actions are being complained of is present as a member, though without the right to vote on this particular issue.

A comparable situation exists in the case of yardmasters, who exercise supervisory authority over the men but who at the same time are employees who bargain with the carrier through a union —which is sometimes the Brotherhood and sometimes an organization composed solely of yardmasters. On approximately half the railroads in the United States the yardmasters are represented by the Railroad Yardmasters of America; yardmasters employed by these carriers may, nevertheless, keep up membership in the Trainmen, with full voting rights and with eligibility to run for any lodge office, though they would not pay the Brotherhood grievance assessment. An anomalous situation exists when a member who wishes to complain of his treatment at the hands of his yardmaster finds that official present as a union member, perhaps even as the presiding officer at his lodge meeting.

The officers of a subordinate lodge include president, vice president, secretary, and treasurer, with the usual duties. The president conducts meetings, enforces the constitution, sees that officers perform their duties, and exercises supervision over the affairs of the lodge. The vice president, in addition to assisting the president and presiding in his absence, is empowered to appoint a minority of all committees, the majority being appointed by the president. The presidency is of less importance than in most unions because the investigation and adjustment of grievances, the most vital business of the organization, is handled by a local chairman—chairman of a local grievance committee of three, the other members being the committee's vice chairman and secretary —elected by the men in each seniority district. A subordinate lodge, therefore, has as many local chairmen as it has seniority districts.

The lodge also has a legislative representative, who keeps the members informed of legislative developments, helps to generate grass-roots pressure when desired, and handles complaints of violation of safety, sanitation, or other laws. To be eligible to serve as legislative representative a member must be a qualified voter, and must have attended at least three lodge meetings in each of the preceding three years and six meetings in the year in which the election is held. A member who notices a violation of state or federal law, or who observes unsafe practices, is supposed to notify the legislative representative. The legislative representative, after making sure of the facts, then refers the matter to the state legislative representative if state law has been violated, and either to the state legislative representative or the president of the Brotherhood if a violation of federal law is involved. In some cases of safety violations the legislative representative may be able to get a representative of the Interstate Commerce Commission to inspect the property. The legislative representative may also get help in enforcing the law from the local chairman. The legislative representative of each lodge is automatically a member of the state legislative board.

It is possible in the Brotherhood for the lodge president or other officer to serve simultaneously as legislative representative or as an officer of the grievance committee. The treasurer customarily serves also as an insurance representative of his lodge; this is not by lodge election, however, but by appointment of the head of the Promotion Department in the Grand Lodge. An insurance representative, who gets a percentage of the first year's premium on any policy that he writes, can usually earn about $50.00 monthly from this source.

In the Brotherhood the convention delegate—the delegate to the Grand Lodge, as he is called—is elected with the lodge officers, and holds office for a four-year term. The delegate must meet special qualifications, however; he must be an insurance member of the union, and must have attended at least three meetings a year in the three years preceding his election, and six meetings in the year in which the election is held. The requirement that the delegate be an insurance member is imposed to meet legal requirements under various state laws, since the convention legislates on insurance as well as on other Brotherhood matters.

The first office to which an active member is likely to be elected is the vice presidency of the lodge, with the line of progression being to the presidency and then to the post of local chairman, the highest that the lodge can bestow. Or one may start as secretary or vice chairman of the grievance committee, and advance from either of these positions to the local chairmanship. An officer who is inattentive to his duties, or who misses two successive regular meetings of his lodge without sufficient cause, may be removed from office (after notice) by majority vote of those members he represents who are present at the next lodge meeting.

The term of office in subordinate lodges, two years until 1958, was extended then to four years, but made three years in 1961 to conform to the requirements of federal law. In the cases of legislative representatives and grievance committees, which are not covered by the federal legislation, the term of office remains four years. To win an election, a candidate must have a majority of the votes cast; if no candidate receives a majority, the lowest man on each ballot is dropped until an election is had. Each lodge may decide whether to elect officers at the lodge meeting or by referendum vote.

Each lodge decides on the scale of payments to its officers, just as it determines the size of the monthly local lodge assessment paid by its members to meet these and other expenses of the lodge. If the seniority district has 400 or more members, it can support a full-time local chairman, and it probably has a sufficiently high volume of grievances to keep him occupied on a full-time basis. Only a handful of Brotherhood seniority districts are large enough for this purpose, or are willing to tax themselves enough to pay a full-time salary comparable to earnings on the railroad. Where the position is not a full-time one, the local chairman is authorized to absent himself from his railroad job whenever his lodge duties require, and bill the lodge for his lost earnings; in addition, the lodge may pay him a monthly salary that ranges, typically, between $75.00 and $150.00, perhaps with an additional sum to compensate him for the car, phone, and other expenses that the position entails. The treasurer, whose duties are quite time consuming, may be paid a comparable monthly salary, with the president and the secretary getting much smaller sums, perhaps in the neighborhood of $20.00 or $25.00 a month to each. A small amount may be added to some of these figures for expenses.

The monthly dues paid by a member represents the total assessed upon him by the various agencies of the union that represent him for different purposes. The Grand Lodge collects a total of $1.50 monthly from each member, of which 50 cents is for grand dues, 75 cents for the protective fund, and the remaining 25 cents for the convention fund. The assessment of the subordinate lodge is usually about $1.00 monthly. There is also a grievance assessment of $1.50 to $3.00 that goes to support the work of the general grievance committee, plus a smaller amount for the work of the local grievance committee, and an assessment of 35 to 75 cents for the state legislative committee. All this adds up to a monthly payment by each member in the neighborhood of $6.00 or $7.00; and the monthly receipt to each member shows how his payment is apportioned among these various funds. For a time after the 1960 convention, dues were even higher, because of a $2.00 special strike fund assessment, levied to raise the strike fund to two million dollars. Insurance premiums, paid monthly, are additional, and depend on the type and amount of insurance that each member chooses to carry. There is also a monthly assessment of 25 cents for tuberculosis benefits. The local treasurer collects all these sums from each member monthly, and sends all but the subordinate lodge dues and the local grievance assessment to the general secretary and treasurer, who maintains accounts for all the remaining funds in the Grand Lodge office. The local treasurer's accounts are audited every six months by the subordinate lodge's finance committee, and, in addition, a Grand Lodge auditor may be sent, at the request of the subordinate lodge or on the initiation of the Grand Lodge, if there is reason to suspect irregularity.

Grievance Handling and the Local Chairman

Much of the business of the lodge deals with grievances against the carrier, with proposals to be negotiated with it, or with problems of safety or sanitation on the railroad. A local chairman who is doing his job properly brings to the meetings his files of active cases, and makes reports to the lodge on the status of each. Where an important claim is involved, he is likely to read his correspondence both with the carrier and with the general chairman (if he was unable to effect a settlement with the railroad superintendent). He also reports on conferences with the superintendent, settlements reached, and amounts distributed; if he has made a personal investigation of safety or sanitation complaints, he also reports on these. The lodge meeting that the local chairman does not attend fails in one of its primary purposes, as is also likely to be the case if the local chairman is present but inadequate to perform the duties of his office.

Railroad labor contracts differ from those typically written in American industry in that they have no termination date. On many roads the basic agreement in effect was written shortly after World War I, following the return of the carriers to private operation. Both unions and management are alert for changes in economic conditions or for collective bargaining developments in other industries that could be used to justify changes in wages, rules, or working conditions. When changes are made, whether by agreement limited to the particular carrier or as part of a national settlement, they are simply added to the original document as supplements or amendments. A railroad contract, therefore, is typically a collection of documents covering a period of 40 years, with the provisions currently in effect on each topic being the most recent ones written with respect to it. All of this makes the task of the local chairman a complex and difficult one.

Although wages are fixed by national negotiations and most other matters by system agreements, there are cases where an individual lodge may negotiate a matter separately with its carrier. Here, a proposal for a change in the agreement originates in the local lodge, which must submit the proposal to a referendum vote of its members or pass the proposal at two consecutive meetings, with notices of the proposed action posted on the bulletin boards at various locations in the interim. If the lodge by either method approves the proposed change, the local chairman, perhaps with the aid of his vice chairman, takes the matter up with the carrier's superintendent. If he fails to negotiate a satisfactory agreement with the superintendent, however, he must seek the aid of his general chairman, since without that official's cooperation he cannot reach management officials above the rank of superintendent.

Because of the complexities of railroad contracts and rules, the handling of time claims and other grievances is a highly technical matter, calling for much greater knowledge than is required in the adjustment of grievances under more typical union contracts. The need to be familiar with the decisions of the National Railroad Adjustment Board, which has jurisdiction over disputes involving the interpretation or application of agreements, adds to the complexities of the union representative's job. The local chairman, therefore, has an extremely difficult position to fill, one that is by no means to be equated with that of shop steward in an industrial union. It takes a man of high caliber, who knows the practices on his road and the key decisions of the Adjustment Board, and who can argue with the skill of a lawyer, to fill with competence the position of local chairman. It takes perhaps two years of experience in the job before one may be said to have learned it well.

Traditionally, in the Brotherhood the lodge meeting was the body possessing jurisdiction over the merits of grievances, with the local chairman its agent for dealing with the railroad superintendent. A member who believed that the carrier had violated the rules to his disadvantage was expected to file a time claim, and upon its denial to bring his grievance, with all the relevant facts, to the meeting of his lodge. If the members present, after discussing the claim, believed it to be meritorious, they authorized the local chairman to present the claim to management. Since the 1950 convention, however, it has not been necessary for the lodge to approve the grievance before the local chairman may act; since 1950 he has been authorized, upon receipt of a claim from a member, to process it with management if he was convinced of its merits, and then report his action to the next meeting of the lodge. This modification of procedure was adopted because of the many small lodges that might go two or three months without holding a meeting, though all local chairmen, if their lodges give them such authority, may follow the new procedure. Typically, a member now goes directly to his local chairman with his grievance, taking it to his lodge meetings for approval only if the local chairman thinks it lacks merit. The grievance process on the railroads, though slow as compared with many other industries, is kept moving by time limits on various railroads. A fairly typical provision requires a penalty claim to be filed within sixty days of the incident or be barred, and allows one hundred and eighty days from the date of the carrier's statement declining payment for the local chairman to handle the claim with the superintendent.

If the local chairman is unable to reach a satisfactory settlement of the grievance with the superintendent of the division or terminal, he reports this to the lodge; (the local chairman lacks authority to carry the case above the superintendent with whom he deals). The lodge then votes either to send the case to the general chairman, for handling at a higher level of authority, or to drop the case, if it appears that merit is lacking or that, for lack of evidence or other reasons, a satisfactory settlement could never be achieved. The tendency is to forward the case to the general chairman, to avoid hard feelings within the lodge; this tendency, indeed, which is apparent at all levels of authority within the union, tends to clutter up the grievance procedure with large numbers of claims that never will be won, and that would have been dropped at an early stage if only someone in authority had the courage to take a firm stand.

Sometimes the lodge may ask the general chairman for his opinion before taking action on the case. The general chairman, presumably, is the official who knows best the rules in effect on the property, and his opinion would carry a great deal of weight with the lodge; the general chairman, in turn, may submit the case to his general committee before communicating with the lodge. In their consideration of the grievances these various officials would be concerned, not merely with whether the case could be won, but with whether it would constitute a desirable or an undesirable precedent. If the decision of the lodge is to reject the grievance, the member may appeal to the president of the Brotherhood, who in turn may ask the general chairman for his opinion before ruling on whether or not the case should be handled with the railroad. Should the member consider the president's decision unjust, he may appeal further to the Board of Directors and then to the Board of Appeals, whose decision is final.

The local chairman who is employed on a full-time basis in this capacity is in a much better position to represent his members in grievances. Not only does he have more time to become familiar with the complex rules and their interpretation, but he can represent his men without fear of the company's displeasure. Otherwise a local chairman who represents his men aggressively may be subjected to severe company discipline in the event that, on his own tours of duty on the road, he violates any of the regulations. However, only about ten of the Brotherhood's seniority districts in the entire country are large enough to afford a full-time local chairman.

The local chairman is called upon to perform many other duties besides handling grievances with management. A worker who is brought up on disciplinary charges by the carrier, whether because of an accident, alleged insubordination, or violation of other company rules, is entitled to be represented at the hearing by someone of his choice, and in the vast number of cases he asks the local chairman to perform that function. Members come to the local chairman for information and advice with regard to retirement benefits, unemployment compensation, or benefits under other railroad legislation. It is part of the work of the local chairman to be informed on the provisions and interpretations of railroad legislation, as well as on collective bargaining agreements and decisions on grievances. A worker who suffers an injury on the job, similarly, may consult the local chairman regarding the procedure to be followed or the sum offered in settlement, or he may ask the local chairman's advice about legal counsel. If the local chairman holds a full-time position as such, he may be asked to perform a wide variety of other services, from visiting the sick to getting a lawyer for a man in trouble, and from advising on investments to arranging a burial or serving as executor of an estate.

The position of local chairman involves considerable authority, in the exercise of which a man is likely to please some of his membership and antagonize others. Where a lump sum settlement involving a number of men is made, for example, the local chairman is likely to apportion the amount among the men involved. The vacation schedule may be made out by the local chairman, who knows the preferences of his men, rather than by management. On a number of roads, to give another example, a rotary board operates for workers who lack the seniority necessary to hold a regular assignment, with minimum and maximum provisions as to the amount of work that they can receive; thus they might be required to earn at least eight days, but not more than twelve, in a period of half a month. If the level of work falls below the minimum, the local chairman notifies the road to furlough the man lowest in seniority, and if it mounts too high he has the carrier recall the top furloughed man. The price of having such authority is the danger of resentment, where men feel that the action taken by the local chairman has operated to their disadvantage.

The importance of the local chairmanship makes the position attractive to ambitious and energetic members of the Brotherhood. It draws attention to a man, makes him well-informed, and gives him an opportunity to become known and to make a record in the handling of grievances. He must be prepared for hard work and constant study, in view of the complexities of the rules with which he will have to deal. For the member who is ambitious for higher union office, however, the local chairmanship is the best place to start. In the small number of cases where the position is a full-time one, it is, needless to say, very attractive for that reason. Even in other cases, however, there tends to be competition for the post, though in very small locals it may be difficult to get a man to serve, since the compensation is limited by the number of members in the lodge and by the assessment, probably a maximum of one dollar a month, that they are willing to pay for this purpose. Sometimes local chairmen resign after a few months because of the disadvantages of the job—the irregular hours, the personal conflicts involved, and the criticism and abuse they have to take from chronic complainers or from dissatisfied members who cannot see the difference between their claims, which may be held invalid, and the claims of other members that were paid.

Opposing Interests within the Lodge

To an operating railroad worker, the most vital factor relating
to the job is his seniority date, which determines his choice of
assignments as well as the order of lay-off and recall. Whereas
with regard to wages and hours, crew consist rules, safety legislation, and the like, the employees have a community of interest
in relation to the carrier, seniority is an issue on which the
clashes of interest occur within the lodge, as each man seeks to
preserve his relative place on the roster from any action that
would place a junior man ahead of him. While in most cases a
worker's seniority date is clearly established, since it is the date
on which he qualified for a particular branch of service, questions
arise when some irregularity occurs in the qualification process,
when workers are permitted to change from one list to another,
or when seniority rosters are merged. Seniority is an area in which
management may take a fairly detached view, since its costs are
not affected by the relative seniority standing of two employees;
let one of the employees feel that an injustice has been done to
him in this respect, however, and the lodge meeting will hear his
complaint, the local chairman and then the general chairman
may be called upon to act, and an adverse decision by the lodge
or the general committee may be appealed by the aggrieved
worker to the president of the Brotherhood and then to the
highest tribunal within the union for such cases.

Four actual cases, selected from the many that have arisen, will
illustrate the kinds of conflicts that arise over the order of names
on the seniority roster. In one case a carrier maintained separate
rosters for freight and passenger trainmen under an agreement
with the Brotherhood providing that, when additional passenger
men were needed, freight trainmen would be given an opportunity to apply before men without prior service on the division
were employed. A freight trainman who made proper application was denied a transfer by the trainmaster, because he had had
only three years of high school work, whereas high school graduation had previously been required. Subsequently, a higher
officer of the company overruled the trainmaster, giving the applicant, at the request of the local chairman, a seniority date as

passenger trainman to conform with his original application. This placed him ahead of four men already on the passenger trainmen's list, one of whom took his complaint to the lodge meeting and got the lodge's support for a place on the roster ahead of the former freight trainman. Since the general chairman supported the carrier's action, the lodge appealed from his decision to the Board of Appeals, which held that the carrier had the right to determine the qualifications for men in passenger service and to relax those qualifications if it so desired.[5]

In another case an experienced yardman who had left the carrier's employment but who was later rehired was not required to pass an examination on the rules or serve the usual days as a student worker. This allowed him to start work ahead of four men without previous experience who had applied before he had, though the carrier, dating seniority according to the applications, listed him after them. The experienced man thereupon filed a grievance with his lodge, which supported him, and the general chairman persuaded the carrier to list the seniority of the men in the order in which they had started work. The four men, appealing from the action of the general grievance committee, were sustained by the Board of Appeals by a five-to-two vote, the Board holding that the original seniority listing followed the practice in which the carrier had engaged in the past.[6]

In still another type of case a brakeman appealed an action of the general grievance committee that allowed conductors to relinquish their seniority as such and return to work as trainman on freight or passenger assignments, after these two rosters were consolidated. As a result the appellant had dropped from position number 3 on the brakeman's seniority list to number 10. His appeal was denied unanimously by the Board of Appeals, on the ground that the practice of which he complained had existed on the property for many years.[7]

The final case in this group of four involved a situation far more serious in its implications for union solidarity. A union member who had been dismissed by the carrier filed a grievance for reinstatement, only to have his lodge vote not to accept his case. He then appealed to the president of the Brotherhood, alleging that the members who had opposed accepting his grievance had so voted, not on the merits of the case, but for personal gain, since they were junior to him in seniority. Of the 20 members present who were eligible to vote on the grievance, 8 were senior to him and the other 12 were junior; the 8 senior men, he asserted, voted to accept his grievance and the 12 junior men to reject it. The president declined to interfere, on the ground that no irregularity in the lodge's action was in evidence, and that under Brotherhood rules the decision as to the merits of a grievance was to be made by the lodge membership. The case was then appealed to the Board of Directors, which urged the assignment of a Grand Lodge officer to investigate the case and submit recommendations to the president. The Grand Lodge officer, following his investigation, recommended that the appeal be sustained on the ground that the carrier had improperly served notice of disciplinary action on the man who was dismissed. The president, adopting this recommendation, sustained the appeal, and instructed the general committee to press vigorously with the carrier the request for reinstatement to the service.[8]

Whereas one effect of the seniority system, as illustrated in the above cases, has been to make each worker watchful of his place on the seniority list, protecting it from any error that would place junior men above him, still another result is to make the younger men, as a group, conscious of their disadvantaged position as compared with the older men. The seniority system is too deeply ingrained for any direct challenge, and the junior men, so long as they get enough work to support themselves and their families, are reasonably content to put up with the disadvantages of low seniority until the passage of time and the retirement of older men enables them, in turn, to pick the better runs and enjoy the higher earnings. Trouble arises, however, when technological advance or decline of demand for railroad service results in short time for (if not furloughing of) the junior men, who then seek a redistribution of the work that will make more time available for themselves. The pressure that they employ takes two main forms: the limitation of the mileage that roadmen may run; and the establishment, and then the lowering, of a compulsory retirement age.

Mileage limitation, raised as early as the 1919 convention, became a serious issue by 1931, when over 40,000 members of the union were reported as laid off. Whereas earlier the chief argument was that the high earnings of "time hogs" injured the union's chances to obtain wage increases, now the issue became the providing of some work opportunities for the younger men. The 1931 convention adopted limitations in terms of mileage for roadmen and numbers of days of work for yardmen, asking the general committees to make these limits effective under their contracts with the carriers. The 1946 convention favored mileage limits, to be determined by the membership on each property, and the 1954 convention, while leaving the number of permissible miles to the judgment of each general committee, made it mandatory that each such committee, at its next meeting, adopt some form of mileage regulations.[9]

Occasionally the conflict between the junior and senior men over mileage limitation may become so acute as to disrupt the functioning of the lodge. Such a case occurred on the Chicago & North Western Railway as a result of loss of business by the carrier to a rival road, which in turn led to a factional alignment in one of the lodges between the older and the younger men. In 1955 the general committee, implementing the mileage limitation action of the 1954 convention, decided to leave the question to the jurisdiction of the individual divisions of the road. One lodge, with the younger men in control, thereupon adopted drastic limitations, far below the amount permitted in the current agreement. On the advice of the president of the Brotherhood, the issue was submitted to a referendum vote of the lodge, but the meeting at which the ballots were to be counted became so disorderly that it had to be closed. Even the presence of a Grand Lodge officer, following this meeting, failed to bring an orderly solution. Finally the president of the Brotherhood ruled that control of the issue, under convention action, was vested in the general committee, which thereupon reversed its earlier action permitting individual divisions to determine the mileage limitations, and placed in effect the provisions of the current system agreement. This action increased the number of permissible miles that could be run, with the result that eight regular jobs were lost and the same number of men cut off the extra board and furloughed.[10]

A situation comparable in some respects arose in 1958 on the Cleveland, Cincinnati, Chicago & St. Louis Railway. While a mileage limitation for men in passenger service was established by the general committee, one of the lodges, beset by a decline of business and the furloughing of some of its members, reduced the allowable mileage to a still lower figure. From this action, a group of the men appealed to the president, whose decision described clearly the difference in interest between the senior and the junior men.

It has been set forth [President W. P. Kennedy wrote to the secretary of the lodge] that there are 15 passenger jobs and 2 extra passenger brakemen in the service limited (11 BRT and 6 ORC), and as a vote of 43 to 15 was returned upon the proposal, it would appear that the membership in passenger service voted almost exclusively against the limitation, while those in freight service almost unanimously supported the limitation. While one seniority list is maintained, the vote would further indicate the control of the earnings of the passenger men by some 60 junior freight and extra men.

The president's decision was that the general committee's limitation would prevail, particularly in view of the fact that the service was interdivisional, with another lodge equally interested in the determination of the issue.[11]

Compulsory retirement, like mileage limitation, is an old issue in the Brotherhood, going at least as far back as 1917. Elderly railroad men in good health have had little incentive to retire, since the seniority system enabled them to pick the assignments that they found least burdensome and most attractive from the point of view of hours and earnings. During the depression of the 1930's, pressure mounted for the passage of a compulsory retirement law to provide jobs for younger men. Passage by Congress in 1935 of retirement legislation for railroad workers, after an earlier measure had been held unconstitutional, encouraged retirement without making it mandatory.

The issue of compulsory retirement was then transferred to the collective bargaining front, where general committees that favored the proposal sought to write such a rule into system agreements. On some roads, as a result, retirement was made compulsory at the age of seventy, and on others at sixty-five. At one of the lodge meetings attended by the author, this issue was one of the main items under discussion. The lodge had just held a referendum vote on the issue, the members favoring compulsory retirement at sixty-five by a vote of almost two to one, with sentiment in favor of allowing a grace period of six months to a year before any agreement negotiated with the carrier took effect. Since the lodge

was the only one of trainmen on the property, it could authorize collective bargaining negotiations without having to work
through a general committee representing other lodges as well.
The proposal for compulsory retirement at sixty-five came under
sharp attack from one of the lodge officers, aged sixty-three, who,
instead, wanted the lodge to act against men who held two jobs.
There were a number of men in the lodge who were known to
have two jobs, including several city firemen and policemen,
whose departmental regulations permitted them to work up to
twenty hours weekly elsewhere. The conflict between junior and
senior men also found expression, though in a less acute form, in
the desire of the younger men to have management put on one or
more extra engines, thereby creating additional jobs, whenever
substantial overtime was being earned.

Still other clashes of interest may occur within a lodge—as
where it must choose between a settlement of a member's grievance of maximum benefit to him as against one that, without
benefiting him very much or at all, may prove of great value to
the rest of the membership. Such a situation arose in the Pittsburgh area with regard to a belt line service set up among five
divisions, with crews assigned to the service on the basis of a
count made every six months of cars moved within each division's
territory. Crew members who were removed from this service on
the basis of an incorrect count earned less on other runs, and put
in claims for the difference, which amounted in the case of one
brakeman to seventy-five dollars. The carrier, admitting that an
error had been made, suggested that the time claims be settled on
the basis of allowing the division to recapture the number of
days lost to it. The lodge accepted the proposal, which gave more
work to the men on the division at the price of closing out the
claims filed by the crew members who were improperly displaced.
On appeal the lodge's action was upheld by the president of the
Brotherhood, on the ground that the lodge members were within
their rights, though he thought it unfortunate that a member
was adversely affected. The Board of Directors, on appeal, upheld
the president, but the Board of Appeals, on a further appeal,
held that the lodge had erred in instructing the local chairman
not to progress the claims for payment.[12]

Still another difference of interest arose within a lodge on the
question of filling temporary vacancies as yard foremen or con-

ductors. The general chairman interpreted the agreement to give such posts to senior yardmen, whereas some of the conductors thought that men who had already established themselves in that rating should receive the work. One of the conductors appealed the case, alleging that the lodge had voted to support the general chairman's ruling because the yard helpers were in the majority, since it takes two of them with one conductor to comprise a crew. In this case the appeal was denied, on the ground that both the wording of the agreement and the practice under it supported the interpretation made by the general chairman.[13]

Clashes of Interest between Lodges

Differences of interest arise, not only within a lodge, but also between lodges, sometimes between men employed on the same railroad and sometimes between different railroads. On the same railroad, differences readily occur when one or more lodges want changes made in the agreement to which other lodges are indifferent or opposed. So far as the performance of work is concerned, the general rule is that the men who hold seniority rights in a particular district or yard have the exclusive right to perform the work of their craft required in that area. Yet occasionally the men of one district, by virtue of a practice of long standing, are considered to have the right to share in work on a portion of the trackage that lies in another district.[14] More typically, disputes arise when a railroad merger occurs, when traffic is diverted from one line or facility to another within the same system, and when interdivisional runs are established. In all such cases the men on each seniority district are alert to obtaining their fair share of the work.

When railroads that have been serving the same area merge, inevitably some of the yards will no longer be used, and the jobs that formerly existed there will disappear. At the same time the work formerly done there will be diverted elsewhere, causing an increase in the volume of work at some locations, though the total volume of employment available will diminish. The district losing the work then seeks an equity in the work done at the expanded facility, which would involve the assignment to its members of a certain proportion of the jobs available there. If no work remains at the old location, the lodge would press for a merger with the lodge holding jurisdiction over the facility to which its work was diverted. Problems may arise as to the terms of merger, however, since the lodge losing the work would want the two rosters merged in order of seniority dates, whereas the other would want the transferred members added at the bottom of its seniority list.

An actual case involving the diversion of traffic within the same railroad system might help to bring the problem into clearer focus. For example, the New York Central Railroad built a new electronic yard at Elkhart, Indiana, and established through interdivisional freight service between Joliet and Elkhart, and between Jackson and Elkhart. The effect was a permanent diversion of Chicago area traffic from the Michigan Central line, a New York Central subsidiary, to the New York Central Railroad –Lines West, and a loss of switching operations formerly carried on at Niles, Michigan. Since the two general committees were unable to agree on an allocation of work, a Grand Lodge officer was assigned to investigate and make recommendations. He recommended that Michigan Central crews get 48 per cent and New York Central-Western District crews 52 per cent of the work in the Elkhart yards, these figures being in proportion to the business handled by each district during the preceding three years.[15]

Disputes over the manning of interdivisional runs are usually settled by awarding to the men of each district work rights in proportion to their respective divisional mileage. In one case, for example, one district comprised 178 miles and another 109 miles, making a total mileage of 287 in the interdivisional run. The work was, therefore, divided on the basis of 62.1 per cent to the larger district and 37.9 per cent to the smaller one.[16] Where the number of trains and hence the number of crew members is very small, a rough division of work, such as two men from the larger division and one from the smaller one, is made initially, with provision that the district not getting its fair share of the work in this fashion can have another of its men relieve the junior man from the other division for a specified period each year to make the mileage allocation come out right.[17]

Still another type of dispute, that caused the loss of bargaining rights for a group of men to a rival union, occurred between yardmen and roadmen, both represented by the Brotherhood, on the Fort Worth and Denver Ry. An agreement had been worked out with the carrier providing that yard crews would be used for switching service at an industry located beyond the line of demarcation between road and yard crews, but with road crews entitled to a specified amount of work within yard limits. Representatives of the Switchmen's Union promised to restore all this work to yardmen if given representation rights, and on this basis won a National Mediation Board election to represent the yardmen. The Switchmen then obtained a court order restraining the road from requiring or permitting road service men to perform the disputed work. Upon intervention by the Brotherhood the restraining order was dissolved, whereupon road crews were reassigned to run off the yard hours due them.[18]

Lodges of men employed on different railroads may conflict where joint service exists, where work is transferred to or from a joint terminal, or where one railroad uses the tracks of another or provides switching service for it. In these cases trouble is most likely to arise when economic conditions produce some significant change in an existing arrangement, so that one group of men can point to established practice and the other group to simple equity in support of their claim to a larger share of a limited volume of work. With employment in the industry declining steadily, important stakes depend on the decision, since the losing lodge may well suffer the lay-off of a number of its junior men. While all these cases arise between conflicting groups within the structure of the Brotherhood, a decision once reached is presented to the carriers in collective bargaining negotiations; the carriers, on the whole, are likely to assent, since the sharing of the work between two groups of men in altered proportions does not add to the costs of operation.

A typical case involving joint service arose in Kansas City as a result of the action in 1945 by two railroads, the Milwaukee and the Kansas City Southern, to coordinate their terminal and yard facilities. Agreement was reached, following the practice that is usual in such cases, to assign yardmen to the joint switching service in a ratio depending on the number of engine hours that each road had worked in the three previous years. This resulted in a formula under which Kansas City Southern men were to get 67.30 per cent of the work, with the remainder going to the

Milwaukee yardmen. Controversy arose six years later when crews were reduced without regard to this formula for allocating work, resulting in proportionately more employment to Milwaukee men. The insistence of the local chairman of the Kansas City Southern that these hours be worked off, and the refusal of the Milwaukee local chairman to agree, resulted in the assignment of a Grand Lodge officer, who recommended that the seniority rosters be consolidated. An appeal from this recommendation, in which the president of the Brotherhood concurred, was sustained on the ground that the carriers should be required to apportion the work as the agreement provided.[19]

Once agreement is reached on a formula for apportioning the work, further disputes may arise over the implementation of the agreement. Thus the general committees on the Monongahela Railway and on the Pittsburgh & Lake Erie, following a long controversy over the manning of joint service, were instructed to apportion the work on the basis of the number of engine hours worked on each property. In order to make the time worked by each group conform to the agreement, from time to time a Pittsburgh & Lake Erie crew was assigned to a Monongahela engine to work off the hours due them. Disagreement then arose as to whether the time that such a crew spent working on the Pittsburgh & Lake Erie property should be counted in the equalization. After that issue was settled a further dispute arose as to whether time should be computed from the time the engine or the last car crossed the line of demarcation between the two properties.[20] Such conflicts between two general committees, it is apparent, can be as stubborn as those between labor and management. In other cases, once the distribution of time in joint service was agreed upon, rival general committees disputed the allocation of daylight hours, the establishment of layover points, or the assignment of vacation work, where it was agreed that all "extra" work should go to the employees of one of the roads.

Another type of dispute arose where a carrier ended an agreement under which its switching on a particular stretch of track was done for it by another railroad. Thus the Pennsylvania and the Chicago and Eastern Illinois jointly built a two-mile branch line in 1917, with an arrangement under which the C. and E. I. did the Pennsylvania's switching on that line for a fee, with the C. and E. I. crews performing all the work. In 1953 the Pennsylvania took over its own work on the branch, and its employees then claimed the right to perform this work. The Board of Appeals held, however, that C. and E. I. men had built their seniority on this work for many years without protest, and were entitled to continue to perform the work.[21]

Much the same considerations are involved when work in joint service is apportioned on the basis of engine hours worked on each road in the preceding years, only to have the proportion of business originating with each road undergo a sharp change in subsequent years. Thus Baltimore & Ohio crews, allotted 31 per cent of the work in a combined yard in 1931 on the engine hours worked in the preceding period, sought to change the formula in 1955 on the ground that two-thirds of the cars coming into the yard now represented Baltimore & Ohio traffic. Their appeal was denied on the basis that the other group of men had built their seniority on the original distribution of work, and could not now be deprived of a type of property right long enjoyed by them.[22]

While the carriers often are willing to accept the proposals for allocation of work made by the Brotherhood in such cases, provided they suffer no disadvantage thereby, sometimes the disputes are stubborn ones, with the Brotherhood in a difficult position because it represents groups of men with conflicting interests. Such a situation arose when the Pennsylvania Railroad and the Pittsburgh & Lake Erie ended an arrangement in 1959 that had lasted for forty-five years under which an industrial switching road performed certain work for them on the south side of Pittsburgh. This resulted in the furloughing of all the employees of the small switching road, which engaged in no other operations. The Brotherhood, which represented the men of its crafts of all three railroads involved, sought to work out an agreement with the carriers that would be acceptable to all. The roads, however, offered a solution that, in the Brotherhood's opinion, would have destroyed the seniority rights of the Pennsylvania and the P. & L. E. men. The Brotherhood refused this proposal, with the result that the twelve men furloughed by the industrial switching road remained without work. The Grand Lodge officer who handled the case could recommend only that time claims should be handed in until finally an arrangement could be worked out to give some protection to the furloughed men.[23]

Relations with the Grand Lodge

There can be no question that the effective power within the Brotherhood structure is in the hands of the Grand Lodge, as the very name, "subordinate lodge," indicates. While it is generally true in American unions that power tends to be centralized in the national organization, this is particularly true of railroading, because of the national character of most collective bargaining since 1931, and because of the provisions of the Railway Labor Act relating to bargaining representation and grievance determination. Whereas in most industries a dissatisfied local may withdraw from its national union and seek bargaining rights as an independent local union, in the railroad industry the National Mediation Board follows system lines for representation purposes, holding, for example, that all the yards of a carrier constitute a proper bargaining unit. Similarly, labor representation on the National Railroad Adjustment Board, which has the power to adjust grievances, is limited to organizations that are national in scope. There is no place on the railroads, therefore, for an independent local union. Usually, however, the presence of rival national unions, to which men on a system may turn in a body, has operated to limit arbitrary use of power by Grand Lodge officers. The election process at conventions, to be described in a subsequent chapter, also exercises a restraining influence on the national officers.

The president of the Brotherhood may revoke the charter of a subordinate lodge for improper conduct; for failure to conform to the union's constitution and regulations; for failure to make its returns and reports; for neglecting to hold at least one regular meeting each month, unless prevented by unavoidable causes; for refusing or neglecting to install a successor to any officer removed by the president; or for failure to bring an officer or member to trial when directed to do so by the president.[24] The president also had power, until recently, to remove subordinate lodge officers for sufficient cause, and to bar them from holding office or representing the Brotherhood in any capacity for an indefinite period. Under the constitution as written in 1960, however, the president can remove a subordinate lodge officer only for violation of the constitution or of his obligation an an officer, and not until he has had a fair trial in his own lodge.

The president also reviews actions taken by a subordinate lodge on appeal by any member. Any decision of the lodge, under Section 79 of the constitution, may be appealed to and reversed by the president, though as a practical matter a president is unlikely to substitute his judgment for that of the lodge unless he believes that the constitution was violated or a serious injustice done. While the president's action, in turn, is subject to appeal, that process, of course, occurs within the structure of the Grand Lodge, and does not operate to return power to the subordinate lodge.

This discussion of the power relationship between the Grand Lodge and the subordinate lodge is in danger of leaving a false impression of the relationship between them, unless it is also borne in mind that a vast amount of information about Brotherhood affairs is made available by the national officers to the local affiliates. There are few national unions in which such a substantial flow of information regularly and routinely occurs. The annual report of the president, which includes that of the assistant president, all the vice presidents, and the national and Canadian legislative representatives as well, goes to the secretary of each lodge, where it is presumably available to every member. This is a detailed report of each officer's activities and decisions, typically running to about four hundred pages. The annual report of the general secretary and treasurer, similarly, goes to each lodge secretary, and his monthly report to each local treasurer. A full financial statement is issued monthly.

The president also sends a monthly circular of instructions, which could be labeled more appropriately one of information, to every officer listed in the quarterly directory, and therefore to every local president, secretary, treasurer, local chairman, and legislative representative. When national wage or rules movements are in progress, a weekly letter on developments goes to all officers in the directory. Twice yearly the reports of the Board of Appeals, containing a detailed discussion of each case, go to every lodge secretary, and at least once a year a general letter goes from the president to every member, summarizing the principal events of the year. Each member also receives **the union's** weekly newspaper, *Trainman News.* An informed membership is one of the necessary conditions of an effectively functioning democracy, though of course it is not the only one; and a member of the brotherhood who wishes to be informed about Grand Lodge affairs has an unusually wide range of material readily available to him.

The position of subordinate lodges in relationship to the Grand Lodge has been strengthened by the formation of local switching associations, composed of local chairmen, in some of the major railroad centers and by the holding of annual meetings of associations of lodges in particular states or areas. Though these various bodies possess neither power nor official function, within the Brotherhood or in relation to the carriers or to public bodies, they are important in that they give the active membership of the lodges an opportunity to meet and exchange views. The resolutions passed at such meetings, while serving merely as an expression of the views of those present, may, nevertheless, serve to mobilize opinion upon matters of importance within the union.

3

The General Chairman and

the State Legislative Representative

Whereas in many unions the division of authority is between local unions and the national organization—and, therefore, the line of progression for the ambitious unionist is from local union office to national officer or staff position—in the Brotherhood there are important intermediate bodies headed by influential officers between the local and national levels. Such intermediate bodies and officers exist both on the collective bargaining front, following railroad system lines, and in the legislative area, following state or provincial lines. The existence of these bodies and positions, whose holders depend for re-election upon the representatives of the subordinate lodges that they represent, helps to keep authority decentralized within the organization. By providing full-time positions, with satisfying authority and attractive salaries that lie beyond the control of the national union heads, this structure helps to prevent the rise of the monolithic political organization, controlled by an all-powerful political figure, such as is found in some unions. At the same time this feature of the Trainmen's structure provides leadership training and experience to active, ambitious unionists, assuring a steady supply of men of proved competence and substantial reputation who are available as candidates for Grand Lodge office, and who are assured of good positions in the union structure even if their bid for national office fails.

The General Committee

On each railroad the chairmen of the local grievance committees constitute the general grievance committee, which meets regularly at least once every four years to elect officers and hear appeals. On some roads an additional meeting on appeals is held every second year. On large roads there may be as many as 75 or 100 local chairmen on the general committee. If fewer than three lodges are located on the system, the chairman and secretary of each local committee function as the general grievance committee. At the meetings of the general committee pending cases are reviewed, votes are taken on the merits of grievances, interpretations of the contract are made, and proposals for new rules are adopted. (On important railroads meetings usually last from three to seven days.) In between regular meetings of the committee special meetings may be called, though the practice is to carry on the work by delegation of authority to the officers or to subcommittees or by use of mail ballots. The officers of the general committee (consisting of chairman, vice chairman, and secretary) are elected for terms of four years. The Brotherhood has a total of 210 general committees operating in the United States and Canada. General committees function similarly in the two countries, except for modifications in collective bargaining procedure to conform to the national laws under which they operate.

Much of the business of the general committee consists of reviewing on appeal claims that the various local chairmen have been unable to settle satisfactorily, and that have been held to lack merit by the general chairman or a subcommittee. Since the full committee meets infrequently, authority is given to the general chairman or to a subcommittee to screen the cases and present those held to possess merit to the highest officers of the carrier. Usually the general chairman, the vice chairman, and the general secretary constitute such a subcommittee—though when there is a large volume of grievances from a single lodge, a subcommittee may be appointed consisting of the chairman and the secretary of the general grievance committee and the local chairman of the lodge involved. If the general chairman or the subcommittee decides that a grievance lacks merit, an appeal from this decision may be taken to the next meeting of the general committee.

Grievances that do not involve time claims are likewise presented on appeal to the general committee. Some such cases involve discipline, ranging from requests for the removal of demerits from efficiency records to pleas for reinstatement in dismissal cases. Other items on the agenda may include the establishment of the Brotherhood's position on interpretations of the rules or efforts to write new rules or change the existing agreement in any way. If the issue is one that can be negotiated with the individual railroad, such as mileage limitation for roadmen, the matter is taken up with the carrier by the general chairman. If the issue is more appropriate for a national wage or rules movement, the general chairman is so advised by the president of the Brotherhood. When such a national movement gets under way, the carrier is so informed and the suggestion is made that conferences on the property be waived to permit joint handling in national conferences, perhaps involving others of the operating brotherhoods as well.

Other matters handled at a general committee meeting include resolutions proposing amendments to railroad legislation or the passage of new legislation; while such resolutions do not establish Brotherhood policy (since policy resolutions are outside the area of competence of a general committee), they serve as expressions of opinion and may influence those who determine legislative policy. Or management may abolish a position on a road which does not have any crew consist agreement, but which operates in states with full crew laws. In situations of this sort the general committee refers the case to the state legislative representative, who institutes legal proceedings if it appears that state legislation has been violated. Still other matters brought before the general committee involve disagreements between lodges, such as alleged diversion of traffic. In addition the committee has its share of housekeeping duties, since it must authorize the purchase of equipment by the general chairman or the hiring of office workers and the fixing of their salaries.

Appeals from the various actions of the general committee may be taken to the president of the Brotherhood, if a question of Brotherhood law is involved (such as whether proper procedure was followed), or to the Board of Appeals, if the merits of a grievance are in issue. If the committee's procedure was proper the president usually upholds its action, on the ground that it has the authority to interpret and apply its agreement. However, if he finds that some interested group within the union was ignored in the handling of a case, he may likely order the case reopened so that its views may be considered.

The General Chairman

The position of chairman of the general grievance committee —or general chairman, as it is usually called—is a key one in the Brotherhood structure. Except for the handful of locals large enough to support a full-time local chairman, the position is normally the first full-time one that is open to an ambitious member of the Brotherhood who seeks to rise within the union structure. On very small railroads, however, there may be too few Brotherhood members to support a full-time general chairman; in these cases the general chairman, in addition to receiving a small salary, is paid from the general committee's funds for the time he loses from work upon its business. Where both the chairman and the secretary of the general grievance committee hold full-time positions, the tendency is for one officer to come from the ranks of roadmen and the other from those of yardmen. Since the general chairman of an important road has an opportunity to build a following and to become known nationally, the post serves as an excellent springboard to Grand Lodge office—particularly since many of the delegates from the lodges on any road are likely to be local chairmen, the very men with whom the general chairman has close working and personal relationships.

While normally there is just one general chairman for the Brotherhood lodges on each carrier, in some cases there may be as many as four or five. Usually the result of mergers, these are cases in which some identity of the formerly independent roads is maintained for administrative purposes. In other situations large railroad systems, such as the Pennsylvania, may be divided by management for administrative purposes, and the union structure follows that of management. According to practice one of the members of the general committee is elected the general chairman, though eligibility extends to any member of the Brotherhood who holds seniority under the committee's jurisdiction. To prevent the election of men who, though popular, lack experience in grievance work, the constitution was amended in 1960 to limit eligibility to members who had served at least four years as chairman of a local grievance committee.

The post of general chairman may be filled either by election by the general committee or, if a majority of the lodges under the committee's jurisdiction so decides, by a referendum vote of the membership involved. Each method of election has its specific advantages and disadvantages. The election by the committee permits a choice by the persons best qualified to judge the ability and experience of the candidates, though it opens up the possibility of undesirable politics and permits the free-spender type to have an undue influence on the results. It may also involve an undemocratic aspect, since the representatives of many small lodges may outvote those of larger lodges with a majority of the membership.

On the other hand, a vote under a referendum, the election system more frequently followed, is a relatively uninformed one, since the rank-and-file member has little knowledge of the competence of opposing candidates. Often he merely follows the advice of his local chairman. Under the referendum method, a man of engaging personality and wide popularity may defeat one who is vastly more knowledgeable and competent in the handling of grievances. In the event that a general chairman is elected who lacks the support of his general committee, the result may be constant friction, weakening the effectiveness of the entire organization. A general chairman, like any other officer or member of a general grievance committee, may be removed from office for cause by a majority vote of the committee.[1]

The office of the general chairman, along with the other expenses of the general committee, is financed by a general grievance assessment upon all members under the committee's jurisdiction. This amount, usually $1.50 to $3.00 monthly, in some cases may be as high as $5.00 or $6.00. Until the passage of the Labor-Management Reporting and Disclosure Act of 1959, the amount of the general grievance assessment was determined by the chairman and the secretary of the committee, with no vote of the full committee or the affected membership required. To bring the Brotherhood into conformity with the new law, the constitution was amended in 1960 to require approval either by the general committee or by a referendum vote of the members; this rule was made applicable in the United States, though not in Canada. The fund thus collected is sent to the Grand Lodge office in Cleveland, where it is maintained separately for the use of the particular grievance committee. The general chairman's bills are sent monthly to the Grand Lodge, and checks in payment mailed from there. The salary of the general chairman, set by his general committee or by referendum vote of his membership, is usually between $10,000 and $12,000 on a large railroad, and may be as high as $14,000.

From the funds at his disposal the general chairman meets the expenses of maintaining his office, including the salaries of officers and clerical employees. Members of the general committee are currently paid $29.62 plus an allowance for expenses for each day spent in the service of the committee, whether in attendance at committee meetings or in consultation, at the request of the general chairman, on cases that may be pending from the lodge. In the event a representation election is held on the road, or if the membership falls too much at any time, the general chairman can put organizers to work; half the cost of paying organizers usually comes from his budget and the other half from the Grand Lodge. If the treasury of the general committee is low, however, the Grand Lodge may meet a larger percentage, or even all, of the expense. If his funds permit, the general chairman may make an appointment himself and assume the entire cost. Though appointments as organizer are made by or in the name of the president of the Brotherhood, when the Grand Lodge pays at least part of the expense, the president usually follows the recommendations of the general chairman, who in turn is most likely to suggest that his key local chairmen receive these commissions. While an appointment as organizer is usually for a short period, perhaps only for several days, and while the pay of $29.62 per day is not unusually high, the appointment carries prestige and constitutes a welcome break from the usual routine. Together with calls to consult on cases, appointments as organizer are political assets to the general chairman; they are bits of patronage at his disposal that help him win the support, so necessary for his re-election, of the members of the committee.

Besides maintaining the Brotherhood's right of representation on the property, the general chairman serves as its chief representative in the handling of grievances that cannot be settled between the local chairman and the carrier's superintendent. Upon receipt of such a grievance from the lodge, the general chairman decides whether in his judgment it possesses merit. If not, he returns it (along with his reasons for doing so) to the lodge, which may appeal his decision to the next meeting of the general committee. If, in the general chairman's view, the grievance is meritorious, he presents it to the carrier's personnel head and attempts to negotiate a satisfactory settlement. In the event of failure he may file the case with the First Division of the National Railroad Adjustment Board, though there is now a delay of five years or more between the filing of a case and its determination by the First Division. For this action, however, the general chairman needs Grand Lodge approval.

If a very large number of grievances accumulates on any one property, a special board of adjustment may be established to dispose of them. Formerly the Brotherhood, like the other railroad unions, could speed up the process of grievance adjustment by taking a strike vote; in this case the President of the United States, following the procedures outlined in the Railway Labor Act, would probably appoint an emergency board to investigate the dispute and offer its recommendations for settlement. This avenue of action has not been open since 1957, when the United States Supreme Court held that, under the provisions of the Railway Labor Act, the railroad unions did not possess the right to strike over grievances pending before the Adjustment Board.[2]

The process of handling grievances is slowed up by faulty procedures within the union. Just as at the level of the subordinate lodge it is easier to pass a poor case on to the general chairman than to risk the displeasure of a member by rejecting his claim, so the general chairman may seek to increase his popularity by keeping cases of questionable merit on the docket. Such a policy is encouraged, not only by political considerations within the union, but also by the fact that the financial costs of the National Railroad Adjustment Board are borne by the federal government. In many instances, moreover, a poor job is done at the subordinate lodge level in investigating cases and assembling the relevant facts. The carriers, which are in possession of the facts, decline to bring them to the attention of the Brotherhood, taking the position, understandably enough, that they will pay claims only where the union can prove its case. The result of all this is that the grievance procedure is clogged with large numbers of cases, many of them of questionable validity and others inadequately investigated, that slow the handling of the cases of genuine merit.

Where a change in a system agreement is sought, the general chairman, after being authorized by a majority vote of the lodges or by a referendum vote of the members affected, takes the matter up with the appropriate officer of the carrier. Once he receives authority to negotiate, he can reach a binding settlement without the necessity of having his agreement ratified; his action is subject to appeal to the president of the Brotherhood, however, if it is alleged that the proper procedure was not followed. If the carrier refuses the requested change, the general chairman requests the aid of a Grand Lodge officer in the negotiations. If a satisfactory settlement still cannot be reached, a notice of an intended change in the agreement may be filed under Section 6 of the Railway Labor Act, which brings the National Mediation Board into the dispute. Under Brotherhood policy the general chairman needs authorization by the president of the Brotherhood to file a Section 6 notice if a national movement is in progress on the issue or if the proposed move would conflict with Grand Lodge policy. In other cases the general chairman files the notice, sending a copy to the Grand Lodge so that that office will be informed when contacted by the National Mediation Board. While the presidential commission appointed late in 1960 was functioning, however, all Section 6 notices required Grand Lodge approval.

If mediation efforts fail, the dispute may go to arbitration or the general chairman may poll the general committee on a withdrawal from service, with a two-thirds vote required to be effective. The general committee, however, cannot order a strike or set a strike date without authorization by the president of the Brotherhood. A referendum vote of the membership may also be taken on the strike proposal, if the union's interests would not be jeopardized by the delay. Though the general committee may be polled quickly by telegram, in urgent cases the general chairman has authority to eliminate this step, though he must always obtain the president's approval before a strike can be ordered. Strike benefits, now $100.00 monthly plus $15.00 for each dependent to a maximum of three, are paid automatically if the procedure required by the Railway Labor Act has been exhausted and if the president approves the strike. The decision to end the strike is usually made by the Grand Lodge officer and a subcommittee of the general committee, though the full general committee may be polled on the issue.

The general chairman is required to prepare a written quarterly report, copies of which must be sent to the president of the Brotherhood and to each lodge and local chairman within his jurisdiction, showing his daily activities, his receipts and disbursements, and the disposition of each claim. In practice the general chairman reports on all grievances to which a file number has been assigned, and not on the many additional matters that he handles successfully by telephone. The reports, which in the case of a large road may run to a hundred or more pages, show where the chairman spent each working day, with whom he conferred, what meetings he attended, and which lodges he visited. The chairman is required to visit all lodges under his jurisdiction at least once during his term of office.

A general chairman who becomes dissatisfied with his treatment within the Brotherhood is in a key position to lead a secession movement, provided he has good contacts and substantial influence in the various lodges on the road and provided also that large numbers of the men are also disaffected, for the same or other reasons. A rival union may appoint him and some of the local chairmen willing to follow his lead as organizers in preparation for a representation election, requiring the Brotherhood to send in a Grand Lodge representative of stature, and also to appoint a number of its adherents as organizers, in order to meet the threat to its representation rights. On rare occasions the general chairman may attempt to form an independent union, though the lack of financial resources and the inability of such groups to get their cases handled favorably by the National Railroad Adjustment Board offers independent unions little chance to win representation elections or to survive if successful in an election.[3]

The personal relations that the general chairman builds with his local chairmen, the president of the Brotherhood, and the personnel officers of the railroad have an important bearing upon his success or failure in the position. If the general chairman is an able man, he will be accepted and supported by his local chairmen. The local chairmen are dependent upon their general chairmen in grievance handling, since they cannot go to a higher railroad official than the superintendent of their division or terminal. The general chairman can help his local chairmen by attending their lodge meetings and giving them support, by calling them to his office on pay for consultation, by suggesting their employment when organizers are needed, and by making special efforts to win their cases; though in most cases the general chairman cannot influence the results much, since the facts determine the outcome, in certain cases, such as those involving discipline, his interest may have an important bearing on the outcome.

The lines of influence run in both directions, however, since the general chairman is either directly dependent upon the local chairmen's votes for re-election, or indirectly dependent upon their recommendation if elections are by referendum vote of the membership. So long as the general chairman serves his lodges well and retains the support of local chairmen and the rank-and-file membership, he is in a secure political position, virtually independent of the international president. Local chairmen, however, may undermine a general chairman by sending him poor cases, by voting for them in the general committee, and by blaming the general chairman for their loss in reports to the lodge. A local chairman who hopes to obtain the general chairmanship for himself may resort to a variety of tactics to discredit the general chairman who blocks his path.

The president of the Brotherhood can help the general chairman by responding promptly to his requests for assistance, by having the Grand Lodge finance organizers when the general committee's fund is low, and by assigning officers of ability and prestige when the help of a Grand Lodge officer is requested. He can help to build up a general chairman by giving him important assignments on national committees and, when the time is ripe, supporting him for Grand Lodge office. Conversely, the president can give a general chairman a minimum of support and recognition, and in some cases may be able to influence the local chairmen to replace him with another candidate for his post. The argument that a rival candidate will get more support from the president may be an important one with some local chairmen, though it is unlikely that many votes will be influenced where a general chairman has a good record of achievement and enjoys good relations with his local chairmen.

The personnel officer of the carrier can help the general chairman by settling cases promptly if they have merit, instead of forcing the chairman to take them to the National Railroad Adjustment Board and suffer the resulting long delays. The personnel officer can also help build the prestige of a general chairman by consulting him before he takes actions that might be disputed, or by turning over to him actions that are clearly a function of management, such as the determination of a vacation schedule. A carrier official is unlikely to be cooperative, however, unless the general chairman deserves his respect. A general chairman who brings in cases that clearly are not supported by the rules, or who argues for contradictory principles in successive conferences, is not likely to receive any favors from employer representatives. As a rule, however, the general chairmen are men of ability who enjoy the respect of the carriers' officers with whom they must deal. Personnel officers are not likely to injure deliberately the prestige of a general chairman, since his successor might be more difficult to deal with and in any event would require a great deal of experience before he knew as much about the system agreement and its interpretation.

A general chairman is not automatically a delegate to a convention, though, like any other member, he is eligible to be elected the delegate of his lodge. If not elected a delegate he may attend the convention as a visitor at his own expense or, if he has business there, such as a pending appeal, his expenses for a brief period may be paid from the funds of his general committee. If he does attend, he is an important political figure, because of his knowledge of national issues and personalities, added to his close personal relationships with the delegates from the lodges he serves. His influence is likely to be greatest with those delegates from his lodges who are members of his general committee.

To be a good general chairman, one must have a great deal of experience in railroad labor relations, combined with a thorough knowledge of the agreement (typically quite complicated) that is in effect on the system, and also of Adjustment Board decisions. He must be a man of intelligence and integrity, and be persevering and aggressive without being offensive. Since the union is a protest organization, he must be a fighter for the workers' point of view, in rules negotiations and in grievance handling. This makes the position unattractive to people who dislike being in conflict situations or who cannot stand constant pressure. Most difficult of all are the situations in which portions of the union are arrayed against each other, as roadmen against yardmen or one seniority district against another. These are among the situations that are most likely to result in opposing candidacies, though the general chairman may minimize the pressures on himself by putting the issue to a vote of the full general committee. While the position is far from an easy one, the alternative is working for the railroad at less interesting and satisfying tasks and at lower pay.

The International Association of General Chairmen

Since 1928 the general chairmen of the Brotherhood have been organized into the International Association of General Chairmen, which functions as an advisory body to the president of the Brotherhood on national wage or rules movements. The Association may adopt proposals as to the objectives of such a movement, and express its views as to the acceptability of the carriers' offer or the recommendations of an emergency board appointed under the provisions of the Railway Labor Act. Actions taken by the Association do not bind the Brotherhood or its president, but serve as an expression of opinion of a body of key men, each of them the chief negotiator for the union with a particular railroad. The opinion of such a group is one that a wise president would be very unlikely to disregard, unless very good reasons exist. The president gets his authority to act for the Brotherhood in national movements by action of the convention, not by that of the Association.

During a national movement the president appoints a wage-rules committee to represent the Brotherhood, and this committee's proposals may likewise be presented to the Association for its views. This committee, which usually includes a number of leading general chairmen, along with Grand Lodge officers, in its membership, would be influenced by the opinions of the Association, though not bound by them in any legal sense. Once such a committee is appointed it has full power to act, though it would not exercise this power without consulting at all key points with the president. The committee's action needs no ratification by the Association, though that body would feel free to express its approval or disapproval of any settlement that the committee accepted.

The International Association of General Chairmen, which holds regular yearly meetings, may also be called into special session if a national wage or rules movement has reached a critical stage. For the 1959 meeting, a fairly typical one, President W. P. Kennedy requested all general chairmen of railroads representing 100 or more assessable members to be in attendance; the sessions, which lasted two days, were attended by 128 members of the Association as well as by 19 Grand Lodge officers and 2 members of its staff. The chief business before the Association dealt with the report of the current Wage-Rules Committee, and with a motion that its proposals be adopted. The Association approved these proposals, deciding that a number of other suggestions for rules changes, offered as amendments, be handled on the individual properties.[4] The Association may also express its views on other key issues confronting the Brotherhood, apart from wage or rules movements. While such expressions of opinion have no binding power, they are listened to because of the power and influence that the general chairmen as a group exercise within the Brotherhood.

The State Legislative Representative

Just as the local chairmen on a road comprise the brotherhood's general committee on the property, so the legislative representatives of all the lodges within a state make up the state legislative board, which meets regularly at least once every four years, and which also holds emergency sessions if legislative business requires them. Traditionally, the members of the state board have elected its officers, though since 1961 the election may be by referendum vote of the membership in the state. The officers are chairman, vice chairman, secretary, and state legislative representative, who together constitute the executive committee of the state board. The executive committee meets prior to each primary and general election to endorse candidates for state office and to recommend to the president of the Brotherhood candidates for the United States Senate and House of Representatives who are considered deserving of endorsement.

Of the officers of the state legislative board, the most important by far is the state legislative representative, whose position is a full-time one in all the large, well-populated states. In these states, the legislative representative attends all sessions of the state legislature, working for the enactment of a legislative program as directed by the state board. Where the position is not full-time, the legislative representative works on a per diem basis, devoting as much time to the legislative interests of the Brotherhood as the legislative board or its executive committee directs. In the states with small Brotherhood membership the legislative representative may merely keep in touch with developments without attending all meetings of the legislature. In states in which the Brotherhood has only one lodge its legislative representative also functions as state legislative representative. The salary of the state legislative representative, which is set by his state board, is at or near the $10,000 figure now in most of the larger states; payment of the salary and expenses of a state legislative representative is made from his state legislative fund, maintained at the Grand Lodge, and accumulated from an assessment on the membership in the state levied by the state legislative board.

While the state legislative representative, as the active lobbyist at the meetings of the state legislature, is easily the key figure in his area with regard to legislation, his authority relates to tactics rather than to policy determination. In this respect he occupies a less authoritative position than the general chairman does in collective bargaining and grievance work. Policy determination in legislative affairs is a function of the state legislative board, which formulates a program, but which must send a copy to the president and obtain his approval before any bills may be introduced. Before the legislative representative may take a position on any pending legislation he must obtain the approval of the state board or of its executive committee; if he is in doubt as to whether a pending bill is consistent with the program approved by the state board, he may have the issue resolved by the executive committee. He may offer an amendment to a pending bill, provided that he informs the president at once of his action. If he wishes to bring in additional members of the state board to help him in his lobbying activities he must obtain the approval of the board and also of the president of the Brotherhood as well.

The state legislative representative plays an active part, not only in the passage of legislation, but also in the enforcement process following enactment. An unsafe condition may exist in violation of state law, as where the required clearance on the side of a track or above it is obstructed. The member observing the violation reports it to his local legislative representative, who in turn communicates with the state legislative representative; the latter sends a complaint to the state agency charged with enforcing the legislation, which investigates and, if a violation is proved, sees that the condition is remedied. As one might expect, there is often great rivalry between the carriers and the railroad unions to influence appointments to key agencies of this type.

A good state legislative representative, besides keeping himself informed on pending legislation, seeks to build personal relationships with as many members of the state legislature as possible. If he is friendly with and respected by them, a word from him when a measure is at the critical stage may sway a badly needed vote. The legislative representative, like any other effective lobbyist, also seeks to learn as much as he can about members of the legislature, and to discover the kind of pressure to which each one may be receptive. The member who represents a district in which a large number of railroad men live will be marked for defeat, if he "crosses" the unions in key votes; or he will be supported for re-election if his voting record is acceptable. A member of the legislature who has few railroad men in his district may, nevertheless, be sensitive to the rail unions' desires if he wants their support for a state-wide office; or he may be anxious for an appointive position from a governor who is on friendly terms with labor union lobbyists. In a district in which a large number of railroad men live, the legislative representative may be on the alert for unionists of ability and personality, whom he encourages to run for the legislature when acceptable candidates are needed.

In all such ventures the lobbyists for the rail unions and the carriers seek to offset each other's activities, the key weapon of the unions being the block of votes they can command, and the strength of the railroads lying in the jobs and wealth at their disposal. Since the legislative influence of any one of the rail brotherhoods is limited, they sometimes form joint committees to pool their strength in any of these conflicts with management. One particular weapon of the carriers, for which the unions have no counterpart, is the offer of advancement into management ranks, as lobbyist or in some other capacity, to a rail union lobbyist with an impressive number of legislative victories to his credit.

A state legislative representative and a general chairman who cooperate can make a very effective working team. Though each is limited to his own sphere of operations, these intersect at a variety of points. A full crew law, such as is on the statute books in about 15 states, means jobs for workers and increases the ability of a general chairman to enlarge and hold his membership on the property. The same is true of safety legislation, or of the situation in which a railroad wishes to abandon a route but must first obtain the approval of a state utility commission. Good relations between lodge legislative representatives and the state legislative representative likewise work to mutual advantage, with the state representative keeping his local representatives well-informed, particularly with reference to matters affecting their local lodges, and the local people responding with the grass-roots pressure needed when bills are at a critical stage. Conversely, where relations between them are bad, a local representative may fail to carry out his instructions, misinterpret the facts in his reports to his lodge, and otherwise injure the effectiveness and reduce the prestige of the state representative. The quarterly reports required of every salaried state legislative representative help to keep the lodges in the state informed of developments of interest and importance to them.

The relationship of the state legislative representative to the Grand Lodge is also of great importance to each. A part-time state legislative representative who feels the need to spend more time at sessions of the legislature may be authorized by the president of the Brotherhood to do so. A full-time representative in an emergency may want the services of a Grand Lodge officer, or he may need additional funds, as for attorney fees, for which he needs the president's approval. Or the president may send the national legislative representative into the state when an important legislative battle nears its climax, or he may ask state representatives to drum up support for a pending national bill, by getting letters and resolutions from the lodges in his area or by going to Washington to put pressure on members of Congress from his state. In all of these respects a state legislative representative and the president may cooperate to mutual advantage and to that of the Brotherhood, just as they may weaken the union's legislative program if they work at cross purposes.

The state legislative representative, moreover, may play an influential role at a national convention with the delegates from his state, particularly with those who serve as local legislative representatives; he does not come as a delegate, however, unless he is elected to that post by his local lodge. Just as the state legislative representative may use his influence at a national convention either to support or to oppose the president, so the latter may use his prestige with the local legislative representatives in an effort to defeat a state representative whom he dislikes. There are limits to his influence, however, since the local legislative representatives will not lightly defeat a state representative who is an effective lobbyist, and who has a record of achievement with regard to the passage and enforcement of legislation.

Often the man who is elected state legislative representative is one who has shown an interest in political matters, as by activity in the Democratic party or, in some states, in the liberal wing of the Republican party. In some cases he may have served in the state legislature; sometimes, indeed, he is the Brotherhood legislative representative and a member of the state legislature at the same time. To some members of the Brotherhood an election as state legislative representative offers an opportunity to serve the membership; other members, however, as in any other walk of life, are more interested in the prestige that the position brings and the benefits that might accrue to them as a result. The post, attractive and satisfying in its own right, may be held on a relatively permanent basis, since the contacts and experience gained on the job are invaluable to the organization, and since a successful state legislative representative tends to be re-elected. Or the post may lead to a political career, to an appointment with the state government, or to a position with the Grand Lodge.

Each of the ten Canadian provinces, similarly, has its own legislative board, composed of the local legislative representatives of the lodges in the province; and each board, in turn, elects a provincial chairman, who also serves on the Canadian legislative board. Under the Canadian legal system, however, the provinces have less to do with railroad matters than do the American states, since the British North American Act confers exclusive authority over the railroads to the Dominion government. Safety, crew consist, and many other matters upon which state governments act in the United States, fall within the exclusive domain of the Dominion authority in Canada. The provincial legislative boards, therefore, have only a limited function to perform, though they meet with their respective provincial governments to propose amendments to such provincial legislation as affects them. Workmen's compensation is the chief area of provincial jurisdiction of direct importance to railroad workers. They are also influenced indirectly by provincial legislation in such areas as minimum wages, vacation with pay, and health insurance; though the provincial enactment does not apply to railroad workers, it has an impact both upon railroad collective bargaining and upon federal legislation written to cover rail employees. The position of provincial chairman is not a full-time one in any of the provinces of Canada.

As in the United States, collective bargaining is more significant than legislative work in Canada, though each type of activity is important in the achievement of the Brotherhood's objectives. Neither at the provincial nor at the Dominion level does the Brotherhood make endorsements of parties or candidates; instead, such political matters are left entirely to the individual members. The union enjoys good relations with the federal government, and likewise with the various provincial governments, regardless of which party happens to be in control.

The National Conference of State
Legislative Representatives

Since 1949, the state legislative representatives have been organized into a national conference which meets biennially, in
election years, to exchange information and coordinate activities
in the legislative and political areas. It is the equivalent, in the
legislative field, of the International Association of General
Chairmen. Conference meetings are attended by the president of
the Brotherhood, the national legislative representative, and
other Grand Lodge officers or staff members. Matters dealt with
include pending federal and state legislation, proceedings before
the Interstate Commerce Commission dealing with mergers or
changes in service, the activities of state commissions, the handling of violations of federal or state law, and political activities,
including endorsements of candidates for president and vice president of the United States. The president of the Brotherhood and
the national legislative representative regularly report to the conference on leading developments in the fields of legislation and
regulation of railroads. Expenses of the Conference are met from
a legislative revolving fund maintained by the Grand Lodge, the
fund being replenished periodically by assessments upon the legislative funds of each state.

Resolutions adopted by the National Conference do not in any
sense bind the Brotherhood; rather, they serve merely as an expression of opinion of those present, and as advice to be considered by the president of the Brotherhood. Yet this does not
mean that their views are of little consequence. As the most experienced officers of the union in state legislative affairs, their
opinions are bound to have great weight when legislative decisions have to be made. A president would be unlikely to disregard a recommendation of the Conference (though in a constitutional sense he may be free to do so), lest he commit a legislative blunder and incur the opposition of an influential group of
Brotherhood officers, whose reports to the membership throughout the country might cause him a loss of prestige, and whose
influence with the delegates at the following convention might
cost him votes needed for his re-election.

The legislative situation, needless to say, may change significantly after the Conference makes its recommendations, so that a measure that seemed possible of passage at one time may appear hopelessly lost at a later date. In such a case the president, while not repudiating the advice of the Conference, might decide, and wisely so, to defer this particular issue while using the legislative influence of the Brotherhood to obtain the passage of other equally needed legislation. As practical lobbyists, accustomed to making decisions of this sort at the state level, the members of the Conference would be the last to criticize the president for such shifts in emphasis within the framework of the Brotherhood's legislative policy.

4

The Presidency

The Brotherhood has had only five men at the national helm since 1885. S. E. Wilkinson served as grand master from that year until 1895, and P. H. Morrissey from 1895 to January 1, 1909, when he was succeeded by W. G. Lee. Lee continued as president, as the position was now called, until 1928, when Alexander F. Whitney took over the top leadership post, which he held until his death in 1949. His successor, W. P. Kennedy, is still the chief executive of the union. While other national unions have shown similar or even greater stability of the top leadership, few have experienced, once the organization had grown in membership and power, the vigorous contests for national office that have been characteristic of the Brotherhood.

In the tradition of most American unions, the Trainmen have a powerful president, one upon whom their constitution confers a very substantial grant of authority. The constitution, in turn, is re-examined at each convention, giving the delegates opportunity to reduce the president's authority if they wish. The president has the power to supervise the union, interpret its laws, determine national collective bargaining and legislative policy, control the avenues of communication within the union, make large numbers of appointments, and play an important role in the union's judicial procedure. One does not readily give up a position of such power, nor the accompanying salary of $27,867.00 —though the salary is far from excessive, in the light of the financial resources of the organization or the sums paid the presidents of other American unions. Unless the president is incompetent or ill, or multiplies enemies by arbitrary and irresponsible actions, it is extremely difficult (verging on the impossible) to prevent his re-election. Though in most unions in this country a powerful president can build a political organization that discourages anyone from even running against him, in the Trainmen it is a rare convention—only four in the last fifteen conventions, covering the period from 1909 to 1960—that has not witnessed a conflict for the presidency. Other unions have had political opposition groups also, but these, typically, were driven out of the union, left in despair to form a rival organization, or dissolved into inactivity when their bid for power was defeated. It is a rare union in which a rival candidate for the presidency is still in good standing by the time of the next convention and in a strategic position to launch another drive for the leading office.

In these respects the Trainmen are unusual, since their history is characterized by conflicts that have not ended with expulsions or the formation of rival unions. The defeated candidate has not only remained in good standing, eligible to run again at the next convention, but, typically, he has retained Grand Lodge office, affording him a strategic vantage point from which to direct his next political effort. Over a fifteen-year period, from 1913 to 1928, Whitney repeatedly contested the presidency against Lee, finally winning the coveted prize in 1928 on his fifth attempt. During his own twenty-one-year period as president, Whitney was re-elected four times, three of these against opposition. This tradition has been continued under Kennedy, who has faced opposition in two of the three conventions in which he successfully sought re-election. While the 1960 convention battle was unusually bitter, the spirited conflict for the presidency was in the Brotherhood tradition, a tradition in which few American unions of power and stability have shared.

Though often challenged, presidents of the Brotherhood are rarely defeated in their bids for re-election. Two sets of factors

call for analysis, therefore: (1) the sources of power of the Trainmen's president that almost assure his re-election; and (2) the
limits on his power or the sources of democratic strength within
the union, that permit political opposition to recur without being crushed or driven out, and that encourage ambitious men
to lead an opposition effort rather than to settle for a secure place
on the administration team and wait for the death or retirement
of the incumbent president. Since a candidate, however ambitious, is unlikely to run unless assured of appreciable support,
it is also necessary to identify the factors that, despite the ac-
cumulation of powers in the hands of a strong president, drive
local groups and active members into open opposition, without
the likelihood that they will suffer serious penalties as a result.

Administrative Powers of the President

Under the constitution of the Brotherhood, the president is
given a broad grant of authority to exercise general supervision
over the union's affairs, and to interpret the Brotherhood's laws
and constitution. The president's interpretation of any constitutional provision is final unless it is reversed on an appeal taken
to the Board of Directors within ninety days; the Board of Directors may also reverse the president's interpretation on its own
motion at its next meeting. The Board's decision, in turn, may
be appealed within ninety days to the convention. This check
on the president's authority may be more nominal than real,
since most of the members of the Board of Directors work under the authority of the president and some may depend upon
his support for re-election—in which case they would be in a
weak position to reverse his action on a point on which he felt
strongly.

The president exercises important controls over subordinate
lodges and over officers of the union ranging from those of subordinate lodges to vice presidents of the Grand Lodge. He grants
charters to subordinate lodges, assigns them their jurisdiction,
approves their by-laws before they become effective, and
can reverse their decisions on appeal. He has ample means of
proceeding against lodges or officers whose actions displease him,
since he can combine lodges or revoke charters for cause after

notice and hearing. Until 1960 he had power, under the union's constitution, to suspend or remove subordinate lodge officers for sufficient cause; the convention of that year limited this power, however, to provide that an officer could be removed only when charged with violating the union's constitution or his obligation as an officer, and then not until he had had a fair trial in his own lodge. The president may obtain and present evidence in order to prosecute members accused of violating Brotherhood rules or principles. Where the president removes a member from office, he has the power to bar him for an indefinite period from holding further office or representing the lodge in any capacity while the order remains in effect. A number of such bans imposed by Whitney were removed by Kennedy after Whitney's death.

The president has even more direct control over many of the Grand Lodge officers, since a number of them, including the vice presidents, work under his direction and in territories to which he assigns them. Unless a Grand Lodge officer enjoys important political backing in his own right, he may owe his election to the president's support, or be dependent upon the president's help in order to gain a higher office. In addition, the president may file charges against Grand Lodge officers who balk him, as Whitney did in a number of cases, provided he can obtain the verdict he desires from the Executive Board, which conducts such trials.

General chairmen and state legislative representatives are in a relatively independent position, since they are elected by and subject to the direction of committees on their roads or in their states, and since their salaries are fixed by their own committees or boards and paid from funds raised in their own territories. Nevertheless, they are also subject to a variety of controls exercised by the president. A general chairman usually depends on the president to appoint the organizers he recommends, to pay half their salaries from Grand Lodge funds, and in some instances to meet a larger proportion of the cost if the general committee funds are low. A general chairman who is ambitious for Grand Lodge office may look to the president for committee assignments that will bring him to national attention, and for political support when he decides to make a bid for international office. A state legislative representative, similarly, cannot obtain additional lobbying assistance without the president's agreement.

Both the general chairman and the state legislative representative are subject to indirect financial controls, inasmuch as their funds are maintained at the Grand Lodge, though the funds are disbursed only as bills are forwarded to the international office for payment. Vouchers submitted by general chairmen or state legislative representatives may not be paid for any of these reasons: because the expenditures are held to be beyond the officer's authority, because per diem is improperly claimed, or because no receipt is attached for a cash expenditure (a receipt is required for any expenditure of two dollars or more). If payment is stopped in this fashion, an appeal may be made to the president, and from his decision to the Board of Directors. All these regulations may be justified on the ground that they assure honesty and order in the handling of the funds, which is doubtless the case; and yet the result tends to diminish somewhat the independence of the general chairman and the state legislative representative.

The president, in addition, has power to levy assessments upon the revolving funds of general grievance committees and of state legislative committees to pay certain Grand Lodge expenses involving grievance and legislative work. Since these funds are maintained at the Grand Lodge, a simple bookkeeping entry transfers the money to funds directly under Grand Lodge control. Though the same result could be achieved by the levy of an assessment, with a failure to pay resulting in disciplinary action, the present system facilitates the collection of such assessments and minimizes the likelihood of protest.

Even more importantly, the president may intervene in the election process, using his influence to defeat a general chairman or state legislative representative whom he dislikes. Here the president controls no votes, and can only seek to persuade local chairmen or local legislative representatives that the candidate he supports could better serve them, in the handling of grievances or in the legislative process, than rival candidates. A general chairman or state legislative representative who has done competent work, and who enjoys the support of the people he represents, can hardly be defeated in this fashion. Some voters, however, may be swayed by the argument that the man desired by the president will get more support from him at critical moments, and so prove of greater help to the membership; and in a closely divided race such influence exerted by the president may well provide the margin of victory. On the other hand, presidential intervention, in addition to causing some resentment, is likely to expose the president to pressure to endorse prospective candidates in subsequent elections.

Collective Bargaining and Legislative Policy

The president also possesses substantial powers over the collective bargaining process. Though each general committee has authority to carry on its own collective bargaining, as a practical matter its ability to do so is circumscribed by the power of the president in two ways: (1) basic money matters and fringe benefits, such as vacation pay, tend to be settled in national collective bargaining, which the president controls through the appointment of wage-rules committees; and (2) if an impasse is reached in bargaining on the individual road, the committee is hampered without the cooperation of the president. Under the terms of the Railway Labor Act, at least thirty days' notice must be filed of an intended change in the agreement affecting rates of pay, rules, or working conditions; and under Brotherhood policy, the filing of such a notice requires authorization by the president if a national movement is under way on the issue or if a conflict with Grand Lodge policy is involved. No strike may be called, or strike date set, without the approval of the president, and strike benefits are paid from a fund maintained at the Grand Lodge. As a result of these various provisions, control over major aspects of the union's collective bargaining is vested in the president.

The practice in the Brotherhood is for a general chairman to request Grand Lodge assistance if the carrier refuses to make desired changes in the agreement. Once a Grand Lodge representative is sent in, the power to make a settlement is transferred to him from the general chairman. Though in practice the two officials usually cooperate, in the event that they disagree as to the desirability of accepting a proffered settlement the decision rests with the Grand Lodge representative, who in turn reports to the president and acts under his instructions. Though the president has authority to direct a settlement that the general chairman and most of the union members think unwise, he would be unlikely to use this power in an arbitrary fashion lest he increase discontent and encourage a secession movement. The president's action in directing that a settlement negotiated with a carrier be signed and put into effect may be appealed to the Board of Directors.

Two unusual cases that have arisen in recent years will serve to illustrate the procedures and rules that govern such matters. In one case, after a tentative agreement had been reached with the aid of a deputy president, the general committee rebelled and refused to sign the agreement. A lodge also expressed disapproval of the proposed settlement and asked that a strike date be set. However, another deputy president assigned to the case reported to the president of the Brotherhood that the settlement was an outstanding one and recommended that it be signed, whereupon the president instructed the deputy president and the committee to sign the agreement. In a letter to the secretary of the lodge, President Kennedy wrote that "Under our law, when a committee as a result of failure to agree with the management requests Grand Lodge assistance, there is vested in the officer assigned the authority to make settlement, subject only to appeal as provided for in the Constitution."

The vice president of the lodge, who was serving temporarily as a member of the grievance committee, refused to sign the agreement and was also charged with trying to interfere with the signing by the other two committeemen. For these actions he was removed from office by President Kennedy and barred from representing the Brotherhood in any capacity during the life of the order. Two appeals were filed with the Board of Directors, one by the lodge protesting the signing of the agreement and the other by the former vice president, protesting his removal from office. Both appeals were denied.[1]

It should be noted that both the president and the deputy president must proceed with caution in a situation of this type, since their insistence upon the agreement, if it proved to be a poor one, would create sentiment against them, on other roads as well as upon this one, that might well be a source of political opposition in the future. The result might also be disastrous for the Brotherhood, since the men, if sufficiently aroused, might leave the organization for a rival union. All these factors contribute to the system of checks and balances that operates within the Brotherhood.

In another case, this time involving bus operators, a national vice president was assigned to assist the general committee in negotiations on contract revision. A difference of opinion developed within the negotiating team; the Grand Lodge officer, the general chairman, and one committee member, convinced that a tentative settlement was the best that could be reached, signed it, whereas the other three members refused to do so. A lodge meeting by unanimous vote supported the position taken by these three committee members. They appealed to the Board of Directors from the action of the Grand Lodge officer and his two associates in signing the contract—the sole issue being his right to do so despite the disapproval of a majority of the committee. This appeal also was denied.[2]

In the area of national legislative activity, the president determines the goals that the union will seek, within the limits of the policies laid down by convention action. Since the latter tend to be broad and general in their nature, ample scope is afforded the president to choose among the various objectives sanctioned by convention action, as well as to decide questions of tactics, such as which of several measures designed to achieve the same general objective merits support, and whether to support or oppose particular amendments. Elected Grand Lodge officers, the national legislative representative in the United States and the Canadian legislative representative, also function in this field, but the president has general supervision over their activities as over most other phases of Brotherhood operations.

In practice the national legislative representative makes recommendations to the president as to a legislative program, within the limits authorized by convention action, that seems attainable in view of Congressional sentiment. The president may consult the Board of Directors, and also the National Conference of State Legislative Representatives, before making a decision, but the decision is his to make. As a practical matter he is likely to follow the judgment of the national legislative representative, who is most closely in touch with Congressional developments. Also, the president is likely to be swayed by the opinions of the other railway labor heads, with whom he sits as a member of the Railway Labor Executives' Association. Many legislative proposals have a very similar impact upon the various classes of railroad labor, and the union heads have learned that their chances of influencing the legislative process are increased if they cooperate. The extent to which the president of the Brotherhood is guided by the collective judgment of the Railway Labor Executives' Association depends at least as much upon his personality as upon the objective legislative situation. Kennedy is likely to accept their judgment and cooperate in joint efforts, whereas Whitney was more disposed to follow an independent line if he could not convince his fellow union heads to follow his lead. Whatever advice the president decides to accept or reject in this area, he has the power to commit the Brotherhood to the national legislative policy that he adopts, within the limits of convention action.

The president, similarly, has the effective power to commit the Brotherhood to the support of candidates for federal office, though in this area, as in others, a wise president is unlikely to use this authority arbitrarily, in disregard of the opinions of other key officers of the union. With regard to the federal Senate and House of Representatives, the national legislative representative submits his recommendations for endorsement, based on voting records in Congress on the key measures in which the union is interested. The state legislative boards, which also watch the voting records of their Congressmen and Senators, submit their recommendations. If the two agree, their choice typically is endorsed in routine fashion at the Grand Lodge office; however, the president, if he wished, could disregard their joint recommendations, as Whitney did in several instances, though Kennedy never has. In the event the state board and the national legislative representative disagree, the issue is sent for determination to the president, whose decision is final.

In the case of candidates for president and vice president of the United States, a recommendation for endorsement is made by the National Conference of State Legislative Representatives, subject to final decision by the president. By the time the conference meets, however, the president's choice may be apparent to all, so that what is a recommendation in form is more likely to be an approval of a choice already made. So far as state offices are concerned, the state boards have the authority to make endorsements without reference to the Grand Lodge, though sometimes they endorse "subject to the approval of the president"—approval that is usually given. The Brotherhood has little or no interest in local politics; nevertheless, local associations of lodges, where these are formed, have authority to endorse local candidates without reference to the Grand Lodge.

The president's authority extends also to the making of contributions to the campaign funds of candidates for federal office. Since under the Taft-Hartley Act union contributions for political purposes may be made only from funds collected on a voluntary basis for such purposes, the Brotherhood has formed the Trainmen's Political Education League in an effort to obtain such funds. The money is collected through the efforts of the state legislative representatives and their state boards, usually on the basis of one or two dollars from each member willing to contribute, and the funds are all sent to the Grand Lodge to be disbursed from there. Decisions as to disbursements to aid candidates for federal office are made by the officers of the Trainmen's Political Education League, whose chairman is the president of the Brotherhood. The state legislative representatives serve as state chairmen of the League. A portion of the League's funds collected in any state must be spent in that state under TPEL rules, and state boards can contribute from their own funds for state candidates if no legal conflicts are involved.

Avenues of Communication

The president also exerts a powerful influence over the avenues of communication within the union. He names the editor of *Trainman News,* the weekly newspaper published by the union, and he supervises its operations and determines its policies in a broad sense. Not surprisingly, the editor features the speeches and other activities of the president, and finds occasion to publish his picture with great frequency. An examination of the issues of *Trainman News* for the year 1958 shows that the president got the featured headline in 22 of the 52 issues, and the second headline on the front page in 5 other issues. A couple of times, indeed, he got both main stories—one a report on his activities and the other an article authored by him. In 15 issues his picture appeared on the front page, usually with those of one to three other union members or public figures. Several issues contained more than one picture of the president and one issue, a sixteen-page one commemorating the seventy-fifth anniversary of the union, published no less than twenty-one pictures in which he appeared. In the case of several issues the president dominated the front page, getting the headline on the lead story, writing one of the two remaining articles, and appearing in the featured picture as well. Often the biggest headline and the only or the leading picture both featured him or his activities.

It should not be assumed that this publicity accorded the president is necessarily illegitimate, or that the president's actions are featured merely because he supervises the editor, as he does other members of the Grand Lodge staff. The paper, after all, is designed to further the interests of the organization that he heads; its policy pronouncements are among the most important news events, from the editor's point of view, and the president makes most of the policy statements, just as he plays a leading role in the union's ceremonial activities. Yet the constant featuring of the president, the reiteration of his name in the headlines and the repeated publication of his picture, gives the incumbent an important publicity advantage over any challenger, and constitutes an important part of the complex of powers and advantages that helps to assure his re-election.

Nor is this the only respect in which the president of the Trainmen enjoys a communication advantage over any possible rival. A constant stream of letters, instructions, reports, and other documents, the great bulk of them in the president's name, goes from the Grand Lodge office to the subordinate lodges. This publicity is of enormous value in popularizing the president's name with the local officers and rank-and-file members.

Even more important, perhaps, were the restrictions (until the last convention) placed upon members or lodges that wished to send material, to which the president might object, through the union. Until 1960, the constitution provided (Section 132) a penalty of expulsion for any member or members who sent circulars to any other member or lodge or circulated reports that were "liable to cause trouble or injure the Brotherhood." This provision, inserted in the constitution to protect the organization from disruption, has seldom been made the basis for disciplinary action in recent years; however, it is readily apparent that the provision could restrict the effectiveness of an opposition candidate's campaign, considering the president's powers to interpret the constitution and the important part he plays in the disciplinary machinery of the union.

Another provision of the constitution (Section 144) required the approval of the president before any circular from a member or a subordinate lodge could be put into general circulation among the members of the Brotherhood. While "general circulation" was never defined, the interpretation being left to the discretion of the president, there was a widespread belief among active members of the union that a circular sent to five or more lodges could be held subject to this provision.[3] One lodge, No. 219 in Chicago, ran afoul of this provision in 1957 when it sent circulars throughout the union without first obtaining President W. P. Kennedy's approval, with the result that its charter was reclaimed and its officers and the members who had attended the meeting that authorized the action were barred from representing the Brotherhood in any capacity. All these bans were lifted within a short time, however, and the charter of the lodge, similarly, was quickly restored. This was the first time in Kennedy's administration that action was taken under this constitutional provision, and it was also the first time that general circulation was attempted without prior approval.

Still other paragraphs of Section 144 provided that the ban on general circulars would not prevent lodges from exchanging proposals to amend the constitution prior to conventions, nor prohibit candidates for office from sending out statements regarding their qualifications. In both these cases, however, there were restrictions upon the type of material that could be sent out, with criticism of or attacks upon any member or officer strictly prohibited. With a candidate for office thus prohibited from criticizing any member or officer in his literature, the effectiveness of his campaign might be limited.

The 1960 convention changed all of these provisions in important respects. The prohibition, under penalty of expulsion, for circulating reports "liable to cause trouble or injure the Brotherhood" was modified to prohibit only the sending of untrue letters or circulars or the circulation of untrue reports. The requirement of presidential approval of general circulars was removed, and in its place the right of subordinate lodges or members to circularize true information among other lodges or members was guaranteed. The prohibition against criticism of other members, in material sent out by a candidate for office, was retained, subject to the limitation that this section could not interfere with a candidate's right under the Labor-Management Reporting and Disclosure Act of 1959 to distribute campaign literature; of course, no union provision could interfere with this right, in any event, since federal law takes precedence over a union constitution. This last-mentioned provision was explicitly made not applicable in Canada.

Appointments

As in any other type of political organization, service is rewarded and loyalty cemented by appointment to jobs at the disposal of the victors. Just as the president of the United States, in his various appointments, is not unmindful of the support that led first to his nomination and then to his election, so the president of the Brotherhood is conscious of the key leaders, influential with groups of delegates at the convention, who made his victory possible. This is not to suggest that he will appoint men to posts for which they lack qualifications, any more than a public official will, since both are anxious for their administrations to achieve creditable records, leading to re-election. All that is meant is that, barring unusual cases where special qualities or experience are needed, the choice for high appointment is made from among those whose political loyalty and contribution are thought to deserve reward.

The president of the Brotherhood has a substantial volume of patronage at his disposal or subject to his influence. With regard to the other leading Grand Lodge posts, such as the vice presidencies, the president, of course, has influence rather than control, since such officers are elected by the convention delegates. The president, however, has the power to appoint whatever number of deputy presidents and organizers are necessary, in his judgment, to meet the needs of the organization. Deputy presidents hold the more important positions, having duties and authority comparable to that of vice presidents. Organizers, of less importance, are appointed when a representation election is pending, when there is dissatisfaction on a property, or when the membership needs rebuilding. Deputy presidents are usually appointed for thirty to ninety days and reappointed if needed; while some may be kept on full-time assignments—3 were so employed in 1959—more typically they work in this capacity for shorter periods of time. Organizers are usually appointed for brief periods, often for from two to five days, the number of days being specified in the notice of appointment. In 1959 the president appointed 28 deputy presidents and 1,344 organizers. In 1958 there were 38 deputy presidents and 2,362 organizers; in the four preceding years the number of deputy presidents who were appointed varied from 78 to 103, and the number of organizers from 1,202 to 1,566.[4]

In addition, the president appoints a number of field supervisors—officers whose duties are to obtain memberships in the union and to sell Brotherhood insurance to new and old members. These officers are not on the union payroll, but are paid on a commission basis on the volume of insurance sold. The appointments, which are for an indefinite period of time, are desirable ones for men who are interested in learning the insurance business and who have the personalities necessary for sales careers. The president also names legal counsel, and there are 21 appointed union counselors in the country.

Until 1959, when the practice was given up as a result of an Illinois decision, the Brotherhood had a staff of investigators, perhaps 40 in number, who were available to legal counsel for use in those accident cases of union members in which investigation by men with practical railroad experience would be helpful. Since 1959 it has been up to each attorney to hire his own investigators, if he thinks any are needed. While most of the attorneys tend to hire members of the Trainmen, some have other investigators on their staffs while still others have little need for such services. The approval of the president is no longer needed for appointments as investigators.

In addition there are staff positions at Grand Lodge headquarters and in the offices maintained in Washington. Approximately 250 persons, about half of whom are women, are employed in the Grand Lodge offices in Cleveland. When men are hired, preference is given to members of the Brotherhood, except where specialized skills are required that members of the union do not possess. Perhaps 100 jobs for men at the Grand Lodge offices are held by members of the union, with another 25, those requiring specialized skills, filled by persons from outside the ranks of the Brotherhood. In addition there are a few posts in the legislative and public relations offices maintained by the union in Washington. As vacancies occur in the Grand Lodge, present staff members are promoted in accordance with seniority and ability, and new appointments are made to the entering jobs through the personnel office, with the approval of the president. Staff members employed in the Grand Lodge offices have the protection of a seniority system and a grievance procedure. Except for those who hold the higher positions, they tend to stay out of factional disputes and to function more like a union civil service group. The president has power of appointment with regard to these positions, therefore, only as deaths, retirements, or resignations occur. Perhaps three to four appointments may be made in an average year.

All of these positions add up to a considerable volume of patronage at the disposal of the president. Yet the president must share his power of appointment with other officers. For the most numerous category of appointments, that of organizers, recommendations made by general chairmen for organizing work on their roads are almost always approved by the president, though the president is not required to appoint the persons they suggest. Vice presidents may also suggest the names of organizers to be appointed in their territories. Sometimes yardmen and sometimes roadmen may be the most effective organizers, depending upon which group of workers is involved in a representation election. If the Switchmen's Union is the opposing organization in an election, men who have had experience with that union, even though some of them may work on other railroads, may be appointed as organizers.

To make the best showing in the election, the general chairman must suggest as organizers those who would be most influential in the area. The failure of the president to appoint his nominees might turn the general chairman into a political opponent of the president. At the same time the general chairman who gets the organizers—typically local chairmen on his property —that he wants may likely be strengthened politically by their support for his re-election, and in turn may be more likely to support the president's bid for re-election. But this is only one factor among many in the relationship between the two men. The general chairman may be disgruntled because he did not receive the president's support for a vice presidential or other Grand Lodge elective position, because he disliked the settlement made by a Grand Lodge representative on his property, because he disapproved of the president's policies in national wage-rule movements or in legislative affairs, or because he did not like the way in which other Grand Lodge affairs were being handled.

The president also has the power to make a number of committee appointments. Some of these, as in national wage-rule movements, bring those who are appointed to national attention, and can be important stepping stones in political careers. In recent years, however, the steady decline of the industry has made such appointments handicaps rather than assets, despite the publicity obtained, because a record of achievement is hard to make in the face of economic adversity and employment decline. A general chairman, moreover, may be weakened by an appointment requiring a long absence from his own railroad. A president also makes large numbers of committee and other appointments in connection with conventions, appointments that bring recognition, often some prestige, and typically small but welcome stipends in addition.

Appeals and Discipline

The president is given a vital role in the appeals procedure maintained by the Brotherhood, a procedure that affords full review of any action taken by any officer or unit of the organization. Nor does the procedure stop with the president; just as any action of a subordinate lodge, a general chairman, or a general grievance committee may be appealed to the president, so in turn any decision of the president may be appealed—to the Board of Directors if a question of Brotherhood law is involved, or to the Board of Appeals if the issue is a substantive one, such as whether a time claim was properly closed out. At all stages of the procedure due process is assured. In the handling of appeals in the president's office, every interested party is asked for a statement before a decision is made, and in important and difficult cases a Grand Lodge representative may be sent out to make a personal investigation and recommendation. The president almost invariably adopts such recommendations.

The problems that flow across the president's desk, upon appeal or protest from members or local lodges, are as varied as the interests and activities of the Brotherhood. Many of the cases involve actions of subordinate lodges, such as the validity of elections to local office or of its actions, taken occasionally, to declare offices vacant. Some issues are procedural in nature, involving such questions as whether the lodge may hold a referendum on a particular issue, or who is eligible to vote. Other actions relate to lodge housekeeping matters, such as refusals to pay bills submitted by officers, or actions reducing their salaries. Questions of the admission, suspension, or expulsion of members likewise occur, sometimes in the form of appeals from the member who is disciplined, and sometimes from individuals who think that the discipline was not severe enough. Other categories of cases that are raised on appeal relate to grievance handling or collective bargaining matters. Members may appeal because lodges refuse to process their time claims or accept other types of grievances, because some action is taken affecting their seniority, or because an agreement is contemplated or reached with the carrier affecting, for example, mileage limitations, the placing of runs in pools as against regular assignments, or a change in terminals.

Other problems raised with the president on appeal relate to actions taken by the general chairman or the general committee. As with the lodge, some problems are procedural and others substantive. In the procedural group are such issues as whether a referendum vote was properly taken, whether a subgeneral committee was properly constituted or properly consulted, or whether a general chairman or a member of his committee has lost eligibility to continue to serve in that position. Substantive issues include the closing out of time claims or other grievances, the determination of seniority dates, the merger of rosters, actions on requests for leaves of absence, the interpretation of agreements, and negotiations with the carrier on such issues as compulsory retirement, mileage limitations, the establishment of extra boards, or the handling of interdivisional assignments.

The problems of these types handled by the president are reported, with his decisions, in his annual reports. An examination of the report for 1958 shows that 63 appeals and similar matters arose. A breakdown of the cases by categories, with the results in each, follows:

TYPES OF CASES	NUMBER OF TOTAL CASES	NUMBER OF APPEALS DENIED	NUMBER OF APPEALS SUSTAINED
Local elections or referenda	30	19	11
Local chairman or lodge—bargaining issues	9	8	1
Local lodge—discipline cases	5	2	3
Local lodge—administrative issues	3	1	2
General chairman or committee—bargaining issues	10	6	4
General committee—procedural issues	3	3	0
General committee—eligibility issues	3	3	0
	63	42	21

The category involving local elections was high because 1958 was a year in which local elections were held. Similarly, in a year involving a major strike, there would probably be a large number of appeals in discipline cases. Except for such issues, however, the distribution of cases as shown is reasonably representative of the types of appeals with which the president must deal in any year.

While the president's power in appeals cases is substantial, there is no evidence that it is exercised in an arbitrary fashion. In general the right of a lodge to act within its area of jurisdiction is upheld, as is the power of the general chairman and the general committee to negotiate with the carrier and interpret the agreement, so long as no irregularities occur. In elections, similarly, the results are not set aside merely because of technicalities, though new elections are ordered where the irregularities were considered important enough to have affected the result or made impossible a free expression of the will of the members. Only a very small percentage of the total number of cases involve politically sensitive issues, as where an active supporter or an opponent of the president is disciplined by his lodge. The issue presented on appeal may be one of guilt or innocence, or it may be whether the punishment was too severe, or not severe enough, in view of the nature of the offense.

Until the passage of the Labor-Management Reporting and Disclosure Act of 1959 the president of the Brotherhood possessed sweeping powers, under Section 9 of the constitution, to "suspend or remove any subordinate lodge officer for a sufficient cause." He was also empowered by the constitution to assemble and present evidence in order to prosecute union members accused of violating Brotherhood rules or principles, and to conduct the trial himself or to deputize another officer to do so. A subordinate lodge officer found guilty could not only be removed from office but, in addition, be barred from representing the union in any capacity for an indefinite period of time. How the powers were used depended on the personality of the president; Whitney used them freely, as Kennedy has used them sparingly.

A subordinate lodge officer may be removed from office for a variety of offenses, including trying to replace the Brotherhood with a rival union, issuing propaganda detrimental to the union, making false accusations against the president or other officers, refusing to sign an agreement when directed to do so, violating Brotherhood laws or principles, or acting in an arbitrary or undemocratic fashion. The officer who feels aggrieved by being thus removed from office may appeal to the Board of Directors. The 1960 convention limited this power of the president by specifying that the president could remove a local officer or committee member only when charged with violation of the constitution or of his obligation as an officer, and not until the accused had had a fair trial in his own lodge. The president may also act against a lodge, revoking its charter for violation of Brotherhood regulations or for other types of improper conduct.

In the case of Grand Lodge officers the president has no power to act, though he may collect evidence and file charges. Cases against Grand Lodge officers are heard by the Executive Board, which is empowered to remove anyone who is found guilty from his office. Whitney filed a large number of such charges during his period as president, resulting in the removal of a number of officers. In 1950 the constitution was amended to limit the president's influence on the Executive Board by providing that its members might not represent the Grand Lodge in any other capacity while serving on the board. Nevertheless, an Executive Board member may feel indebted to the president for past support or think the president's influence vital for his own future advancement; and in such cases, depending on the personality and ambitions of the Board member, the desire of the president might be a factor in the decision. More desirable types of Board members, needless to say, would make their decisions solely on the facts in the case. Kennedy has filed no charges against Grand Lodge officers during his twelve years as chief executive.

Checks and Balances within the Union

This description of the authority of the president may make him seem invulnerable, and indeed the odds are greatly in favor of his re-election. Yet, as has already been pointed out, the tradition of the Brotherhood is one of opposition, and often spirited opposition, to the return of the president to office. Clearly there must be factors, in the industry or in the union, that permit or encourage the expression of opposition in political form, and that make the Brotherhood somewhat different in this respect from most successful and established American unions.

The president of the Brotherhood, like the head of any other union of substantial size and power, must make a large number of decisions, many of which are bound to displease some members of the union. Let him fail to satisfy the basic expectations of the membership for effective representation and protection in their relations with their employers, or use his powers in an arbitrary fashion, and discontent will spread in the membership ranks. For every active member whom he appoints to a desirable union post, thereby cementing his political allegiance, there are apt to be a number of disappointed candidates, who might be encouraged thereby to join an opposition group. Able, experienced, and ambitious seekers for the highest office in the Brotherhood have seldom been lacking in its history. Yet considerations of this sort would hardly be lacking in other unions as well; the question, therefore, is not whether some reasons for dissatisfaction exist, but rather what factors, in the case of the Brotherhood, encourage the expression of this dissatisfaction in political form.

One of these factors is the relatively high degree of job security that trainmen enjoy. Although employment has been declining steadily in recent years, the men of long years of experience, who tend to be most active in the union, are protected by the seniority system against the danger of lay-off. Except in the case of very marginal roads, they have little fear that their employer will go out of business—even bankruptcy would mean only the replacement of one management group by another. In railroading there is more job security among wage-earners than among members of management. So long as a man does his work properly, he has little fear of ever being forced to look for another job, and, therefore, he feels a substantial degree of independence in relation to his union officers. In industries characterized by short-term employment, on the other hand, a worker can scarcely afford to alienate a union official whose favor may help him get another job when his present one gives out.

Added to this is the nature of the union security system on the railroads. The fact that the union shop was illegal on the railroads until 1951, and that since that time a worker could satisfy a union shop requirement by joining any national union admitting workers of his craft, has given trainmen a degree of independence of their union officers that members of few non-railroad unions have enjoyed. Let a union head make himself too unpopular with his men, and they may join a competing union. Let the national president antagonize a popular general chairman, and the latter may lead his men into one of the rival unions, winning bargaining rights for it from the Brotherhood. This avenue of escape may be closed, in part, if the projected merger of the Conductors and the Trainmen becomes a reality.

Another important factor is the distribution of authority within the union. General chairmen and state legislative representatives who enjoy the support of the lodges and the men they serve have little fear that a president can cause their defeat. Holding jobs that satisfy in both an economic and psychological sense, they can afford to speak and vote their convictions. The presence of a relatively large number of such desirable posts, independent of the patronage system controlled by the president, gives ambitious men a chance to acquire experience and to learn leadership skills, and assures the union of an ample supply of able and tested men, apart from those on the administration team, who are qualified candidates for Grand Lodge office. By the same token, the man who is defeated for re-election to Grand Lodge office does not have to make the choice, so common in other industries, of returning to an undesirable job in the plant or leaving the industry. More typically, the defeated Grand Lodge officer can exercise his seniority to obtain a favorable working assignment at good pay, preparatory to running again for a full-time union position.

Within the Grand Lodge itself there are two important factors that deserve examination, the diffusion of power among a variety of boards and the nature of the convention. These factors will be explored in subsequent chapters.

5

Presidential Styles

In the fifty-two-year period from 1909 to 1961 there have been only three presidents of the Brotherhood—Lee from 1909 until his defeat by Whitney in 1928, Whitney from then until his death in 1949, and Kennedy from that time until the present. Though the powers of the office have remained substantially the same over this half-century period, there are interesting differences in the way that each of these three men has used his power. These differences reflect personality and character rather than any changes in the objective situation, inside or outside the union, with which the three men were confronted.

Certain characteristics, of course, they shared—indeed, some almost certainly must be shared by any man who rises to the top of a militant organization of a couple of hundred thousand members. One must have intelligence and drive, the ability to speak well and to inspire people to follow one's leadership, the aggressiveness and perseverance necessary to win collective bargaining concessions from management, determination in fighting internal political battles, and organizational ability to fashion and reward a political machine that will win elections within the union. Without qualities such as these, no one would rise within the ranks of the Brotherhood to become its head, or long survive in that position if he obtained it by some fortunate combination of accidents. Within these limits, however, differences among the three men, in personality and in styles of presidential leadership, are readily apparent, with Lee and Whitney tending to exhibit minor variations within the breed of hard-headed and hard-fisted union presidents and Kennedy representing a more permissive and conciliatory type of personality and union leadership.

The discussion that follows, while paying attention to personality characteristics, will center attention upon the way in which each president has used the authority of his office in political struggles within the union. Sometimes such struggles bring out the worst traits in a man, since power and perhaps political survival may depend upon the outcome. A president with any tendency to make arbitrary use of his power is perhaps most likely to do so in a political struggle, just as tempers are readily lost and intemperate statements are likely to be made by all concerned. The focusing of attention upon the political aspects of a president's behavior is likely to show him at his worst, and find him exhibiting markedly different characteristics from those shown in the great bulk of less controversial situations in which he must daily act. Yet in an analysis of the structure of power and the political life of the union this is the major point of interest. One must bear in mind, therefore, that, without intending to be unfair to any officer, the study focuses upon that aspect of his behavior likely to show him in the least flattering light.

The Brotherhood under Lee, 1909–1928

Lee was an able, aggressive, and forceful person, smart and capable in his handling of Brotherhood affairs, and an effective public speaker. In his personal relations he was gruff and blunt, a "diamond-in-the-rough" type. There was a toughness, with a touch of arrogance, about him, that attracted some and repelled others. He was a militant fighter for economic benefits for the union membership and led the Brotherhood through the long and arduous fight for the eight-hour day, which the railroad unions achieved in 1917 by federal legislation as a nationwide strike was about to go into effect.

Even before he became the union's chief executive officer, Lee's aggressive qualities had made him a leading figure within the union and a target of attack by those who disliked him or had rival ambitions. While he was still assistant grand master—a post later called assistant to the president—and, therefore, second in command to P. H. Morrissey, he was attacked as "Czar Lee" in an anonymous circular distributed at the 1907 convention. Lee was elevated to the top leadership post by the Board of Directors in January, 1909, upon Morrissey's resignation, and elected to a full term as president, as the position was now called, at the May, 1909, convention, without opposition. For the next two decades the Brotherhood was torn by a bitter contest for power between Lee and Whitney, a contest in which no possible weapon was overlooked but during which both men were kept continuously in high Brotherhood office.

Whitney first attracted national attention as general chairman of the Brotherhood on the Chicago & North Western Railway, an office that he resigned upon his election as one of the vice grand masters in 1907. For the following two decades the men were bitter rivals, though Whitney as vice president had to work under Lee's direction. Whitney's repeated efforts to gain the presidency were not caused, as sometimes happens, by loss of membership, collective bargaining failures, deterioration in wages or living standards, or other setbacks making the membership restive and dissatisfied. On the contrary, the period was one of almost steady growth in membership and influence of the Brotherhood, except for a rather sharp decline in membership between 1919 and 1922, when all railroad unionism was on the defensive.

To some degree there was a difference in philosophy and tactics between the two men, Lee being the more conservative in political and economic outlook, while Whitney, in addition to holding a more progressive point of view in economic and political affairs, was a more vigorous fighter on behalf of the union's membership. Yet these differences became most marked toward the end of Lee's presidency, when he was no longer a well man. It happened, also, that Lee had been a yardman and Whitney a roadman, and to some extent support for the two men divided along these lines. To a degree a sectional interest was also reflected, in that Whitney's support centered in the Midwest, where he lived, whereas Lee's main area of strength lay in the East. For the most part, however, the internal political conflict is to be explained in terms of two ambitious, vigorous, and determined men, who repeatedly clashed in the struggle for political leadership.

At the 1913 convention, the first at which Whitney contested the presidency against Lee, the two men clashed over the form of liability compensation to be endorsed by the Trainmen, the key issue debated at the convention. Lee supported a proposed federal workmen's compensation act, under which uniform payments for deaths or injuries would be made without suit; Whitney, however, took the lead in arguing instead for preservation of employers' liability provided by the 1908 federal law, under which larger payments could often be obtained subject to the risk of litigation. Much to Lee's chagrin, the convention adopted Whitney's position. Whitney then challenged the presidency, losing to Lee by a vote of 446 to 394. Lee, in return, backed a candidate who unsuccessfully sought to defeat Whitney for the third vice presidency. After World War I the two leaders differed over continued support of the Plumb Plan for public ownership of the railroads, which Whitney continued to favor after Lee's enthusiasm had cooled. They disagreed again in the presidential campaign of 1924, when Lee supported Calvin Coolidge on the Republican ticket while Whitney, along with most railroad unionists, was an ardent supporter of the Progressive candidate, Robert M. LaFollette.

The feud between Lee and Whitney reached a climax at the Toronto convention of 1922, the most disorderly in the history of the Brotherhood. Fights occurred between members of the rival factions and police intervention was necessary to restore order. The Brotherhood had recently erected a headquarters building in Cleveland, and Whitney suspected that the price to the union had been padded, with a share of the extra sum finding its way into the pockets of some Grand Lodge officers. Early in the convention a vote of confidence was given to President Lee and other Grand Lodge officers who supported him, and Whitney was ordered to apologize to them. Later, Whitney took advantage of his absence from the convention to confer with an accountant, formerly employed by the union's Board of Trustees, seeking evidence to support his suspicion that graft had been involved in the financing of the new building.

Whitney's trip, in turn, became the occasion for a statement presented to the convention by the general secretary and treasurer and the full membership of the Board of Trustees. After reviewing Whitney's efforts over the years to discredit Lee and other officers, the statement called upon the convention to try Whitney and remove him from office if he was found guilty of improper behavior. At the climax of a disorderly session, punctuated with threats to call the police, the convention, by a vote of 454 to 451, with 17 present but not voting, decided not to conduct such a trial.[1] Later in the convention Whitney again challenged Lee for the presidency, losing in a close contest. A Lee supporter then defeated Whitney for the second vice presidency, but Whitney was elected to the fifth such post, defeating another candidate who ran with Lee's blessing.

This series of election results is illustrative of the behavior of Brotherhood convention delegates in factional conflicts. Though factional leaders and their most loyal supporters may wish to defeat rival leaders for any leading position, a number of delegates will not follow any such vindictive policy. In part this represents a desire to keep the talents of an able man at the service of the Grand Lodge, and in part it reflects the influence of the seniority system that is ingrained in the thinking of railroaders. To their way of thinking, one who has served the Grand Lodge faithfully for many years is not to be deprived of any Grand Lodge post, simply because a rival leader seems better qualified to run the union as president.

Early in 1928, when the post of general secretary and treasurer became vacant, Whitney was appointed by the Board of Directors to fill the unexpired term. At the convention later that year, Whitney finally won the presidency in his fifth effort, defeating Lee by the narrow margin of 486 to 462. By this time Lee was suffering from cancer, its stage so far advanced that many delegates did not expect him to live until the following convention. In addition to those who supported Whitney because they liked his qualities of leadership, because they had been antagonized by some of Lee's decisions, or because they had made a political deal with Whitney, there were a substantial number who did not want a sick man at the helm, or who preferred to elect a president at the convention rather than have the Board of Directors fill an unexpired term. Had Lee's health remained good, it seems very unlikely that Whitney could have been elected over him. Lee then ran successfully for the office of general secretary and treasurer, the post that Whitney had just vacated, winning it in a fairly close vote. A year later he was relieved of his post because of his illness, and shortly afterward he died.[2]

Lee could fight his own membership upon occasion as vigorously as he fought the carriers or his factional opponents within the union. In 1920 there was serious dissatisfaction within the ranks of the Brotherhood, the result of a steady rise in the cost of living. Workers in various other industries had won pay gains by the threat of strike, while the railroad brotherhoods, and especially the Trainmen, had failed to move vigorously, and as a result had lost the confidence of large numbers of union members. A minor incident in Chicago sparked an outlaw strike, which spread rapidly throughout the Chicago switching district and reached other areas as well. The leaders of the Trainmen, alarmed, denounced the strike as a violation of their contracts, threatened the strikers with expulsion unless they returned to work promptly, and then recruited workers elsewhere to break the strike. Lee canceled the charters of 92 local lodges, with 30,000 members, while Whitney, under Lee's general direction, took charge of the union's efforts in Chicago to break the strike. There is no evidence that Lee and Whitney differed in their attitude toward the outlaw strikers. Under the combined pressure of management, union officials, and the government, the strike collapsed; participants in it were rehired only as new employees, losing their accumulated seniority, while the active rebel leaders were refused re-employment. The strike left a heritage of bitterness that plagued the ranks of the switchmen, in Chicago and elsewhere, until the retirement of the men who had either lost seniority as a result of the strike or had served as strikebreakers.

Lee's bluntness and pugnacity, when fully aroused, were shown in a letter that he sent in July, 1923, to one of the vice presidents of the Brotherhood, Val Fitzpatrick. Charging that Fitzpatrick had told union members, at the 1922 convention in Toronto, that Lee, instead of suffering from cancer, had "a dirty dose of . . . ," Lee called his fellow officer "the nearest to a dirty, double-crossing cur that I have ever had dealing with." Also charging Fitzpatrick with treachery to the union and to him during the illegal strike of yardmen in 1920, Lee promised, upon his return to duty following an operation, to file charges with the Executive Board against Fitzpatrick and to "tell you, in plainer language than the law will permit me to put in a letter, what I think of you." Fitzpatrick resigned the following month, shortly before Lee's return to his Brotherhood duties.

Shortly thereafter, Lee acted similarly with regard to another Brotherhood officer, M. J. Murphy, who had been chief clerk to the president for many years before being elevated to a vacant vice presidency, at Lee's suggestion, by the Board of Directors. Murphy, according to Lee, had said that Fitzpatrick's statements about Lee's illness were accurate, and in addition had gossiped about the personal life of a former grand master of the Brotherhood. In a letter to Murphy in October, 1923, Lee called him a "character assassin," and offered him "redress either personally or in accordance with Brotherhood laws—if you have the courage to do either." Murphy also resigned a few weeks after receiving this letter.[3]

The Brotherhood under Whitney, 1928–1949

Whitney was easily Lee's match in ability, toughness, and aggressive self-confidence. He was a strong and dynamic type of leader, militant in his relations with railroad management, equally determined where government was involved, and similarly impatient of opposition within the ranks of the Brotherhood. A natural leader, he was prepared to accept responsibility and make decisions, however difficult the situation, showing imagination and an ability to accept and develop new ideas. A man of quick temper, he made his own decisions and brooked no opposition from anyone, turning quickly even against friends of long standing who sought to balk his plans. Yet he ran the union according to the constitution, insisting that its provisions bound him as they bound everyone else. If he could not convince the other railroad unions of the wisdom of a particular course of action, he did not hesitate to lead the Trainmen into a fight by themselves. He was careful of appearances as well as of reality; lest he be accused of too friendly relations with management, he was careful not to meet with railroad officials in the absence of other Brotherhood representatives. Because of his vigorous leadership in advancing and protecting the interests of his members in disputes with management or government, Whitney enjoyed the support of the bulk of the membership, who were willing to overlook his dictatorial tendencies within the ranks of the organization.[4]

His supporters within the union asserted that he enforced the constitution impartially, obeying its provisions even where he questioned their wisdom and filing charges against any officer or member guilty of violations. His critics, on the contrary, argued that he watched his enemies within the union carefully, filing charges against them whenever he caught them in a violation; or that he constantly assembled and recorded evidence of improper practices, making them the basis for charges whenever anyone crossed him. Whichever of these views was the more accurate, there is no question that Whitney's personality left few people neutral with regard to him; union members tended to be either strongly for him or strongly against him.

Whitney was conscientious in his work for the Brotherhood. A man of tremendous energy, he arrived at the office early, worked steadily all day, and frequently left the office loaded down with more work for the evening hours. Always in a hurry, he was abrupt with persons who merely wanted to pass the time, dismissing with little ceremony friends who dropped in for social visits, and sometimes antagonizing them and turning them into enemies as a result. He insisted that every other person on the Grand Lodge payroll similarly do a full day's work every day. Yet he never organized his staff properly; he tried to keep personal control of details as well as of policy, and was unwilling to delegate enough authority to run the office efficiently.

Careful in the handling of his own funds, Whitney was equally scrupulous with regard to Brotherhood money, building up the treasury and insisting that every dollar spent bring its full return. He tolerated no loose or improper handling of Brotherhood funds, and would not permit any officer or employee to overcharge the union, as by asking a larger per diem allowance than that to which he was entitled. As such cases were brought to his attention, he demanded the return of any money improperly collected, and filed charges against any who would not comply. In such matters he was as quick to act against his friends and supporters as against his enemies within the union. Aware that people might seek personal favors in return for paying his bills, he insisted on paying for his own meals and hotel rooms.

Whitney made some far-reaching reforms in the operations of the union. Until he became president, the insurance department had functioned on an assessment basis, levying upon policy holders in order to pay claims. This system was actuarily unsound, particularly in view of the advancing average age of the membership, and shortly after assuming the presidency, Whitney took the leadership in changing the insurance program to a legal reserve basis. While this was a necessary step, giving the membership assurance that reserves would always be available to pay claims, some element of political risk was involved, since premiums were sharply increased for many policy holders. Whitney modernized the insurance accounting system at the Grand Lodge, changing it from a time-consuming hand method to one that utilized modern office equipment. He also took the leadership in the early 1930's in invoking mileage limitations to provide more work opportunities to junior men.

The character of Whitney's leadership in relations with the carriers and the government was shown during the 1946 wage and rules dispute and the nationwide strike of the Trainmen and the Engineers that year. All the rail brotherhoods, in that first postwar year, had joined to demand substantial pay raises and also rules changes. At the critical point in the negotiations, 18 of the 20 unions agreed to arbitrate the pay issue and to drop the demand for rule changes. The Trainmen and the Engineers remained adamant, however, with the result that an emergency board was appointed to investigate their case and offer recommendations for settlement. Both the emergency board and the arbitration board awarded pay boosts of 16 cents an hour, though the national pattern for industry as a whole called for 18½ cents.

Dissatisfied with the recommendations and with President Truman's compromise proposal, the Trainmen and the Engineers embarked upon a nation-wide strike on May 23, despite the fact that Truman had seized the roads several days earlier. As a result, Truman asked Congress for drastic legislation enabling the president to defeat a strike called in an essential industry following governmental seizure. Almost simultaneously, the two unions settled the strike on Truman's terms. Charging that Truman's proposed measure was fascistic, Whitney was quoted as saying that he would spend the entire treasury of the Brotherhood, totaling $47,000,000.00, if this was necessary to defeat Truman for re-election in 1948. This was quite impossible, as Whitney well knew, since the great bulk of the money, segregated in the insurance fund, could not be used legally for any other purpose. In 1948, however, Whitney actively supported Truman for re-election.

Following the strike, charges were filed against Brotherhood members, perhaps 50 to 60 in number, who had worked in various capacities during the strike on roads where Trainmen contracts were in effect. Many of these members were expelled, their expulsions involving, at first, the loss of their union insurance policies. This was a serious penalty, especially to those who because of age or disability found it difficult, or perhaps impossible, to obtain other insurance. Under pressure on this issue, from court cases and complaints to the insurance commissioners of various states, the Grand Lodge changed its policy, accepting insurance premiums from the expelled men. The union convention in the fall of 1946 revised the rules of the insurance department to provide that members who were expelled from the Brotherhood under charges could retain their insurance if they so desired. The union showed its opinion of such former members, however, by issuing them receipts printed on yellow paper.[5]

Whitney's inability to brook opposition within the union put the democratic traditions and structure of the Brotherhood to a severe test. During Lee's 19 years as president Whitney had spearheaded the opposition, receiving the support of a substantial segment of the local leadership, without either he or they seriously running afoul of the disciplinary machinery of the union. Whitney, however, was quick to take disciplinary action against those who opposed his measures, resulting in the removal of a large number of officers who displeased him. Typically, his first tactic, when officers opposed him, was to send investigators into their areas to see whether they had violated any of the rules of the organization, using for this purpose a variety of staff officials or union members whose actions he could control.

When Whitney found evidence of violations he took disciplinary action, removing subordinate lodge officers and often banning them for an indefinite period from representing the Brotherhood in any capacity. In those days a trial could be conducted either in the Grand Lodge offices, if the president so chose, or in the area where the accused lived; and it was conducted by an officer designated by the president. Or the president was empowered in his discretion to take summary disciplinary action, removing a subordinate lodge officer without affording him a trial. In either case the person removed from office could appeal, but whether or not he would receive an impartial hearing and a fair decision depended in large part on the political relationship between Whitney and the members of the Board of Appeals.

Whitney also tried to exert control over the general chairmen, removing several who would not follow his leadership, where a basis for disciplinary action could be found, and in other cases seeking to influence the outcome of elections. In at least one case a general chairman whom Whitney removed from office was re-elected by the men on his road, who might have followed him to another union had Whitney sought to impose further disciplinary measures. To influence elections, of general chairmen or state legislative representatives, Whitney often sent in field supervisors and organizers, ostensibly to increase membership, oppose the efforts of a rival union, or sell Brotherhood insurance policies. It was not difficult, while engaged in these tasks, to tell Whitney's views of the rival candidates to the key men. Particularly in small towns, organizers and field supervisors enjoy substantial prestige; the membership, enjoying great respect for Whitney, might support his choice, either because they respected his judgment or because they wanted a general chairman who could get support from the president of the Brotherhood when this was needed.

Charges against Grand Lodge Officers

Whitney was equally quick to file charges against Grand Lodge officers whose actions displeased him. Though his success in such moves depended upon the verdicts of the Executive Board, Whitney's record was an impressive one. His peak year for such activity was 1941; on March 5 he filed charges against the union's national legislative representative, on March 11 against one of the vice presidents, and on December 2 against four of the seven members of the Board of Appeals. In due course all of the accused were found guilty and removed from office by the Executive Board by three-to-two votes, with the same two members of the Board dissenting in all the cases. This record suggests that factors other than an objective review of the facts of each case influenced, or perhaps determined, the decisions.

In the case of the four members of the Board of Appeals, Whitney charged that they had failed to comply with the law and policy of the Brotherhood, that they had not performed their duties properly, and that they had encroached upon the jurisdiction and authority of the president. Whatever the technicalities on which they were removed from office, it seems clear that their real offense was in reversing some of Whitney's decisions raised with them on appeal. Three of the four had been elected at the 1939 convention as anti-Whitney men, giving Whitney's supporters control by the narrow margin of a single vote; then David Wagner, one of the original Whitney group, alienated by some of Whitney's actions, switched sides, creating an anti-Whitney majority. Finding this situation intolerable, Whitney collected evidence against them until, with the aid of a friendly majority on the Executive Board, he could have them removed from office. Wagner then became active in the Conductors, leading fights against the Trainmen that cost the union substantially in money and effort.

Perhaps the most important case in which Whitney filed charges against Grand Lodge officers occurred in 1947, when two of the three members of the Board of Trustees were removed from office. In 1946, P. J. Baumberger and E. C. Bassett had been elected to the Board of Trustees, a body chosen by the convention to supervise the financial affairs of the Brotherhood, to see that Grand Lodge officers discharged their financial duties faithfully, and to prefer charges to the Executive Board against any officers thought guilty of irregularity in or neglect of their financial duties. In an interesting reversal of roles, Whitney filed charges against Baumberger and Bassett, charging them with having obstructed efforts of the president, injured his reputation, and otherwise violated their obligations as officers of the Brotherhood. What the charges really amounted to was that Baumberger and Bassett, in their actions as trustees, had opposed some of Whitney's policies and actions.

Behind the charges, and the actions of the two trustees that led to them, lay an interesting political situation. Baumberger and Bassett, both of whom had been Whitney supporters at an earlier time, had been elected trustees in 1946 as anti-Whitney candidates. The convention also voted to make the positions of the trustees, who previously had been paid on a per diem basis, full-time ones with annual salary. No sooner had the convention adjourned than a controversy arose over the salary that the delegates had intended. Whereas Baumberger and Bassett believed that the formula for Grand Lodge salary increases adopted by the convention produced an annual scale of $11,775.00 for each of the trustees, Whitney took the view that the figure came to a mere $8,072.00. Holding this amount insufficient for the chairmanship of the board—the one position on the board filled by a supporter of his—Whitney sent a circular to all the delegates to the recent convention asking them to vote on a proposal to raise this one salary to $11,000.00, giving them no opportunity to express themselves on the other two salaries. The vote returned by the delegates overwhelmingly endorsed his proposal. Baumberger and Bassett, in the meantime, had protested Whitney's circular ordering the referendum vote. Another issue arose regarding per diem claims submitted by the two trustees, Whitney taking the position that the claims were illegal.

The conflict reached a climax several months later, when Whitney prepared to establish a Public Affairs Institute as part of the public relations program sponsored by the Brotherhood. Needing the support of the trustees for extraordinary expenditures, such as this was, he obtained the approval of the two trustees who were available for consultation and left for Washington with an initial $10,000.00 check with which to set up the Institute. When the third member of the Trustees, Baumberger, returned to Cleveland, he and Bassett, who now changed his vote, wired Whitney withdrawing their authorization for the expenditure. The two trustees took the position that the $10,000.00 check for the establishment of the Public Affairs Institute represented a donation of funds to another organization, which under Brotherhood rules required a two-thirds convention vote. Whitney, on the other hand, argued that the check was the necessary first step in the implementation of a convention decision. It was this difference of opinion, along with the embarrassment that Whitney suffered, that led to his filing of the charges, as a result of which Baumberger and Bassett were removed from office by the Executive Board. The decision also had the effect of barring the two men from serving in any representative capacity within the Brotherhood until so authorized by the president. They appealed from this decision to the next convention.

By the time the convention met in 1950 Kennedy was president; (Whitney had died the previous year). The key vote was taken on Baumberger's appeal, which under the constitution required a two-thirds vote if the decision of the Executive Board was to be reversed. This Baumberger failed to get, though he did receive 60 per cent of the votes; 639 delegates voted to reverse the decision of the Executive Board and 419 to sustain it, with 706 votes required to change the Board's decision. Kennedy showed his sentiments, however, by announcing that he would remove the restrictions on Baumberger and Bassett at the close of the convention. The delegates expressed their resentment at the outcome of the vote by amending the constitution to provide that only a majority vote of the convention would be necessary in the future to reverse an Executive Board decision or to amend the constitution. They also upheld the appeal of Baumberger and Bassett on the question of their salaries.[6]

The convention also inserted into the constitution a provision prohibiting members of the Executive Board from representing the Grand Lodge in any other capacity while serving on that board. Since Executive Board members did not hold full-time positions with the Grand Lodge, being paid only on a daily basis while they were hearing cases, it may have been possible for a president to curry favor with board members by giving them other Grand Lodge assignments. The convention action was designed to prevent such a practice, as the one in which Whitney had engaged, in the future, thereby seeking to assure greater objectivity and impartiality in the hearing of future charges against Grand Lodge officers. The outcome of the Baumberger-Bassett case, therefore, was a substantial move by the Brotherhood in the direction of greater democratization, in curbing the exercise of autocratic power such as Whitney, with the aid of the Executive Board, had been able to engage in.

As he grew older Whitney became increasingly suspicious that other Brotherhood officers were planning to run against him for the presidency, and he spared no effort to destroy anyone who, in his belief, harbored this ambition. Some of the charges that he filed against Grand Lodge officers for relatively minor offenses might owe their explanation to this deep-seated fear on Whitney's part. His suspicions also attached to staff members and Grand Lodge employees, for fear that they might be disloyal to him and be working in the interests of an ambitious Grand Lodge officer. Whitney was said to have had his own informer or informers among the staff, with the result that employees were hesitant to make uncomplimentary remarks about him lest the remarks be reported to him.

Yet even under Whitney a strong tradition of independence remained. Only in 1935, of the four conventions at which Whitney was re-elected, was he returned to the presidency without opposition. At the 1931 convention H. B. Wells sought the presidency, and both in 1939 and 1946 C. H. Smith contested the office. Whitney won all these elections easily, the closest vote being in 1939, when Smith received 393 to 546 for Whitney. Both times Smith then ran successfully for one of the vice presidencies.

Despite the substantial vote cast for Smith, particularly in 1939, there is agreement that he enjoyed little support in his own right, except in his home state of Texas and in neighboring states; the bulk of his votes were always anti-Whitney rather than affirmatively pro-Smith ballots. In part this was due to resentment against Whitney's dictatorial tendencies, and in part it was a reflection of the widespread dissatisfaction of railroaders during the depression years, when large numbers of workers were laid off. Regardless of economic conditions or the personality of the chief executive, moreover, there are always some members who turn against the administration because they are disappointed office seekers, because they disagree with some of the many decisions the president has made, or because they think that greater concessions should have been obtained from the employers. All of these factors helped to swell the Smith vote. In addition there were a number of former Lee supporters who were never reconciled to Whitney as president, and who would cast their votes for anyone who challenged him.

Whitney never filed charges against Smith, either because he could find no evidence of violations or because he did not regard Smith as a serious contender for the presidency. Some of those who were close to Whitney in his later years assert that he had more fear of Kennedy, one of his principal supporters, on the ground that Kennedy's popularity within the organization, combined with the difference in their ages, made Kennedy a man more likely to win substantial convention support. Others question this, pointing out that Kennedy was elected to various of his Grand Lodge positions, including the post of general secretary and treasurer, with Whitney's support.

It is a rare union in which a vigorous and strongly entrenched president such as Whitney faces opposition for re-election, and a rarer one yet in which his opponent in such a contest successfully obtains another national office at the same convention. Thus the same pattern that was evident in the years of the Lee-Whitney feud reappeared during the period of Whitney's presidency. In the light of Whitney's dictatorial tendencies, this is evidence of underlying factors that strongly favor democratic practices within the union.

The Brotherhood under Kennedy

Upon Whitney's death in July, 1949, the Board of Directors chose W. P. Kennedy, the union's general secretary and treasurer, to fill the unexpired term. Two other officers also had support for the presidency, D. A. MacKenzie and C. H. Smith, who had twice contested that post against Whitney. MacKenzie, who was nearing retirement age, was unwilling to take on the constant traveling that falls to the lot of the president. He and Kennedy, therefore, pooled their strength, under an arrangement whereby Kennedy was to get the presidency and MacKenzie the post of general secretary and treasurer, which Kennedy would be vacating. Once Kennedy had received a majority of the votes, the Board of Directors made the election unanimous.

Kennedy, who had been the Brotherhood's general chairman on the Milwaukee before becoming a Grand Lodge officer in 1935, had served the Grand Lodge successively as trustee, as vice president, and, since the 1946 convention, as general secretary and treasurer. While he was vice president, he had been in charge of the Super-Promotion Department, handling representation disputes in all parts of the country, in addition to participating in a number of wage or rules movements. In these capacities he had worked with union leaders throughout the country, building up a network of friendships that were to prove important political assets during the remainder of his union career.

It would be hard to find a greater contrast than that between Kennedy and Whitney, in personality as well as in their ways of running the organization. Where Whitney was blunt and aggressive, Kennedy tended to be soft-spoken and diplomatic, seeking to lead rather than to dominate, and to reconcile differences through reason rather than to impose a solution through force. Whitney was satisfied to be feared and obeyed, whereas Kennedy wanted also to be liked. Among Whitney's greatest failings were those in personal relations, precisely the area of Kennedy's greatest strength. People tended to react strongly to Whitney, becoming devoted followers or bitter enemies; Kennedy, however, called forth fewer reactions at either extreme. Whereas Whitney was always on the job at the union office, dominating every detail of Grand Lodge business, Kennedy maintained an office in his home town of Minneapolis, in addition to the Grand Lodge headquarters in Cleveland, and was at his best in the field, visiting the lodges and speaking at dinners. If Whitney gave his department heads too little authority, Kennedy was criticized for giving them too little direction, for allowing too many decisions to be made for him rather than by him.

Far from being a rigid disciplinarian of the Whitney type, Kennedy was inclined to overlook minor infractions of the union's regulations. Whitney had removed a large number of subordinate lodge officers and banned them indefinitely from representing the Brotherhood; Kennedy promptly restored their rights to all these members (who numbered over 125), and has himself in only a very few cases removed local officers and imposed political restrictions on them. He has recalled the charter of only one lodge as a disciplinary measure, restoring the charter soon afterward, and has never filed charges against Grand Lodge officers.

Whereas Whitney fought hardest under pressure from the carriers or from the government, Kennedy was more inclined to adopt a conciliatory rather than a belligerent approach. One can hardly imagine Kennedy in the sort of bitter battle with the president of the United States in which Whitney engaged in 1946. In 1950, after Kennedy had succeeded Whitney, the Trainmen and the Conductors rejected the recommendations of an emergency board and prepared for a strike. President Truman again seized the roads, whereupon the heads of the two unions announced that they would gladly operate the trains until the dispute was settled. The truculence so characteristic of Whitney, in his activities within and without the union, has never been exhibited by Kennedy.

In the legislative field, similarly, Kennedy has been a team worker, supporting the position on legislation adopted by his fellow union presidents on the Railway Labor Executives' Association—rather than taking an independent position if he could not win them to his way of thinking. Under Kennedy there has not been the almost continuous strife, with the carriers, with government, or with other unions, such as tended to be the case in the Whitney period.

This does not mean that Kennedy escaped opposition or criticism. At the 1950 convention C. H. Smith ran again, but received only 229 votes to 824 for Kennedy. Smith then ran for the first vice presidency, being elected over five other candidates. At the 1954 convention Kennedy was re-elected unanimously. Beginning about 1956, however, there were increasing rumblings of dissatisfaction with his leadership; he was criticized in various quarters as insufficiently militant in his relations with the carriers, for being a follower rather than a leader, for not adhering strictly enough to the provisions of the union's constitution, and for spending the union's funds too freely and for his own political advantage. Gathering momentum, this dissatisfaction coalesced into a movement of political opposition.

The Convention Issue, 1956–1959

It seems strange that a man of Kennedy's temperament should be subjected to bitter attacks, centering around alleged dictatorial tendencies and violations of provisions of the union's constitution. Yet such was the case for a period of three and a half years, from the middle of 1956 until January, 1960, when a leading issue before the Brotherhood was the holding of a regular convention. Following the postponement, by referendum vote, of the convention which normally would have been held in 1958, Kennedy resisted growing pressure favoring the holding of a convention.

His actions, from the point of view of his own political fortunes, seem hard to explain; if the convention had been held when originally scheduled, it seems unlikely that any substantial opposition to his re-election would have developed. With the postponement, however, he appeared to his political opponents to be attempting to lengthen his period of office without exposing himself to the risks of another election; his tactics had the result of coalescing an opposition group, giving them issues with which to appeal for membership support, and thus creating a movement that almost brought about his defeat. His course of action might be explained by an unwillingness to admit a mistake or to change a course of action under pressure, by the underlying financial situation of the union, or by a fear that a convention would lower the eligibility age of officers to sixty-five, thereby making it impossible for him to remain as president (since he reached that age in 1957).

There is some danger in treating the convention fight in detail, in that it may give a partial and perhaps distorted view of Kennedy's behavior as president. It is doubtful that any other issue would make him appear so arbitrary in the exercise of his power. Yet the issue was the most important to arise during his presidency, with important consequences for the internal political life of the union. The convention fight also showed in clear relief the balance of powers and pressures operating within the Brotherhood that at times permit the top officers to determine union action, and that at other times allow the lower ranks of officers, aided by the active rank-and-file membership, to take the control of the organization's policies into their own hands.

The convention issue had its origin at a meeting of the Board of Directors on June 14, 1956, at which a decision was reached unanimously to hold a referendum vote of the membership on the desirability of postponing the convention scheduled to be held in 1958. The referendum circular, marked Special Circular No. K-21, referred to the high cost of conventions—two and a half million dollars in 1954 and almost that in 1950 and in 1946,—the absence of a convention fund, and the need for an assessment of fifteen dollars on each member, payable one dollar monthly, if a convention were to be held. The ballots carried in parentheses next to the "YES" box the explanation, "means to postpone convention. Pay no assessment." Adjoining the place for a negative vote were the words, "means don't postpone convention. Pay assessment." Returnable to a firm of public accountants in Cleveland, the ballots provided spaces directly under the voting lines for the member's signature, address, and lodge number.[7] The membership voted to postpone the convention by a vote of 103,-448 to 6,126, with 2,431 ballots being incomplete or otherwise invalid.

The circular raised several questions, one of which was the authority under which it was issued. The constitution of the union states (Section 4) simply that "The Grand Lodge shall meet quadrennially in the city to be selected by the Board of Directors," without any provision for postponement, by referendum or otherwise. There were two precedents for postponement by referendum; one, on a ballot authorized by the Board of Directors, occurred during the war year of 1942, when the Office of Defense Transportation of the federal government, in the interests of the war emergency, restricted the use of passenger transportation facilities for non-essential purposes. While there could be little disagreement with the 1942 action of the Board of Directors, it remained a question whether the Board had the constitutional authority to exercise in normal times the authority that it had assumed in a war emergency. On one earlier occasion, at a time of badly depressed economic conditions throughout the country, a convention had been postponed for one year, from 1934 to 1935, following a referendum vote; but in this case the decision of the Board of Directors to hold a referendum had been authorized by a resolution adopted at the previous convention.

In justification of its action the Board cited the language of Section 19 of the constitution, authorizing it "to consider all matters referred to it," though it would be a strange construction that would allow the Board to enlarge its scope of authority merely because the president or some other officer had improperly referred a matter to it. Just a month before the Board of Directors decided to submit the convention postponement to a referendum vote, Kennedy had expressed in a letter the opinion that it lacked authority to do so, unless perhaps many lodges requested such action.[8]

Another question raised by the circular and referendum was the absence of discussion of the issue, so far as communication from the national office was concerned, before members were required to vote. The action of the Board of Directors was taken in June, 1956, more than two years before the next convention was scheduled to meet. Certainly the problem of financing a convention was a long-term one that could have been anticipated and discussed at any time. *Trainman News,* the official newspaper of the union, is issued weekly and mailed directly to each member. Under the circumstances it seems, at least to the outside observer, a questionable procedure to have members vote on such an important matter as postponement of the convention without any earlier or current reference to the issue in *Trainman News.*

It should be noted, however, that it has not been union policy to use *Trainman News* for controversial issues, on the grounds that the paper goes to non-members, including management officials, and is kept on file in public libraries, where anyone may read it. Instead, the policy is to publish such material in the monthly circular of instructions, which goes to the leading officers of each subordinate lodge. Under the practice followed in this instance, discussion of the referendum could have occurred during the sixty-day period allowed for returning the ballots, during which time each lodge presumably would hold two regular meetings. Because lodge attendance is normally small, however, it was probable that the bulk of the members returned their votes without having had the benefit of a discussion of the issues in the union press or under union auspices.

Still another question was the manner in which the issue was presented to the membership. The wording of the ballot—"YES—(means to postpone convention. Pay no assessment.)" and "NO—(means don't postpone convention. Pay assessment.)"—emphasized the financial saving, which the body of the circular estimated at fifteen dollars a member, that could be achieved by a negative vote. While conventions are expensive and must be paid for by the membership, they are also the instrument for determination of policy and election of officers by delegates chosen by the membership. The postponement of conventions, besides extending the terms of the officers, deprives the membership of the opportunity to formulate the policies by which the officers will presumably be guided in the period to follow.

Finally, it was a highly questionable practice to require the member to sign his name, address, and lodge number on the ballot itself, thus destroying the secrecy of the ballot, so far as the firm of public accountants was concerned. The union heads did not learn how each member voted, since the firm of accountants furnished the Grand Lodge only a tabulation of the votes, showing the number cast for or against postponement by the members of each lodge. Yet full secrecy of the ballot is an important consideration that unions should seek to safeguard. While the names of voters had to be checked against the membership list, to make sure that only authorized voters cast ballots and that there was no multiple voting, this could as easily have been achieved by having the signature and the other required information on the envelope containing the ballot, with the valid ballots removed before being counted in order to safeguard secrecy. The Trainmen are familiar with this method of safeguarding secrecy in written ballots, since Section 85(b) of the constitution requires that it be employed whenever local lodge officers are elected by referendum.

It should also be recognized, however, that the inactive membership of the union, ineligible to run for the post of delegate and concerned with protection on the job rather than the Brotherhood's internal affairs, may be disposed to omit conventions and save the cost, in the absence of a pressing need. Local officers, absorbed in the union's internal life and hoping to be chosen delegate, may take the contrary view, particularly in view of the length of conventions and the generous payments to delegates for their services.

Not long after the referendum results had been announced there was a stirring of resentment among a small part of the membership, and the beginning of a movement for the calling of a special convention. One letter of protest from a lodge secretary said that members "had become bitter because they have fallen victim to a cheap psychological trick." [9] The letter was addressed to General Secretary and Treasurer W. J. Weil, who had voted for the referendum, though he later reversed his position and subsequently led the opposition movement against Kennedy.

Clyde M. Titler of Lodge 703, and also the members of Lodge 498 of Altoona, Pa., appealed to the Board of Directors from the decision of the president that announced postponement of the convention. Kennedy refused to recognize the appeals, pointing out in his letter to Titler on January 31, 1957, that the referendum had been authorized by the Board of Directors, which could hardly review its own action.

In the meantime, moves were being made by some groups in the union to obtain a special convention, under the provisions of Section 24 of the constitution, which provided for publication in *Trainman News* of all requests for a special convention, with a vote upon the issue in each lodge if petitions from one hundred lodges were received within a sixty-day period after the first such petition arrived. The first effort in this direction was made in November, 1956, when an anonymous circular, mailed from Chicago, was sent widely throughout the country—in violation of the constitution—urging lodges to request the calling of a special convention. Lodge 1028 then adopted a resolution to this effect, but Kennedy ruled its action illegal because it resulted from an anonymous circular.

On March 30, 1957, Lodge 219 of Chicago mailed a printed circular to the secretaries of all local lodges, urging the passage of resolutions favoring the calling of a special convention for four purposes—one of them being revision of the clause in the constitution relating to age eligibility for union office. The 1954 convention, taking the first such step in the union's history, had made members who had reached the age of seventy ineligible for election or appointment as Grand Lodge officers, and some groups within the union were now urging that the age limitation be set at sixty-five. At this time the president was just a few days short of sixty-five, and several other Grand Lodge officers were older.

Kennedy reacted promptly and vigorously to the mailing of this circular. The action of the lodge had clearly violated Section 144 of the constitution, which required approval by the president of the Brotherhood before a circular from a subordinate lodge or any member thereof might be put into general circulation within the union. Since no such approval had been requested, the circular was an illegal one. Following a hearing conducted by another Grand Lodge officer, Kennedy reclaimed the lodge's charter, transferring the membership to a neighboring lodge, and declared the former officers of the lodge, and also the members who had attended the meeting where the illegal action was taken, ineligible to hold any elective lodge office. Soon afterward, however, he restored the lodge charter, also making the former officers and members again free to hold office.

Lodge 703 of Brownsville, Pa., sought, by following the provisions of the union's constitution, to do what Lodge 219 had attempted to do in disregard of constitutional provisions. It requested approval from Kennedy of the sending of a general circular, urging the lodges to pass resolutions favoring a special convention. Kennedy, however, denied the request,[10] partly on the ground that the membership of the union, including that of Lodge 703, had voted overwhelmingly in the referendum to postpone the convention, and partly on the ground that the expense of circularizing the union's entire membership would be prohibitive to a lodge of under 150 members.

During this period, Lodge 507 of South Boston, Mass., adopted a resolution asking for a special convention, and requested publication of the resolution in *Trainman News,* as provided by Section 24 of the constitution. This section provides that, if one hundred lodges petition within a sixty-day period, asking that a special convention be called for a specific purpose, all the lodges shall be asked to vote on the issue. Under the terms of the section, all such requests for a special convention, together with the purpose for which the convention is desired, shall be published in the first issue of *Trainman News* after the request is made. Kennedy ruled, however, that the union paper would not publish Lodge 507's resolution unless one hundred similar resolutions were received within a sixty-day period. With the columns of *Trainman News* thus closed and with approval of a general circular refused to Lodge 703, it was difficult to see how the communication necessary to obtain the required number of lodge resolutions could take place.

In August the members were notified that, beginning with November, 1957, each member would be assessed twenty-five cents a month for a convention fund, to be used to defray the cost of the convention scheduled for 1962. The idea had originated with one of the lodges, which pointed out to Kennedy that the members had shown themselves by the referendum vote to be opposed to a large assessment in a short period of time; since the large sum necessary to finance a convention had to be accumulated somehow, the lodge suggested that a small monthly assessment would not meet with objection. This proposal was adopted by the Board of Directors and put into effect. (While it seemed eminently sensible to raise the necessary funds in advance and by small increments, some members may have resented the fact that they were assessed for a convention fund so soon after having voted to omit a convention in order to escape an assessment.)

In the early fall of 1957, officers of subordinate lodges were informed that new elections for their posts, as required by the constitution, would be held that November. The only exceptions were local grievance committees, which were to be elected a year later, and convention delegates, who were to hold office for another four-year term, unless otherwise decided, because of the convention postponement. While there was no reason to extend the terms of the other local officers—indeed, to do so would have been a direct violation of the constitution—some of the local officials may well have been irritated because their terms had expired, whereas the convention postponement had operated to extend automatically the terms of officers of the Grand Lodge.

The Impact of State Insurance Laws

In the meantime, the movement for a convention proceeded on two separate legal fronts, one involving appeal to state insurance officials and the other the filing of a court suit to compel the calling of a convention. A typical state insurance law, while exempting representatives of fraternal insurance organizations from the fees that must be paid by commercial insurance agents, provides that conventions and election of officers must be held at least once in four years, though often this provision is waived for organizations that limit their membership to a single hazardous occupation. All these provisions applied in Ohio, in which the main office of the Brotherhood was located, and under the laws of which the union's insurance department had been incorporated. The issue also arose in a number of other states, including Pennsylvania, West Virginia, Wisconsin, Oregon, Georgia, Alabama, and also in Canada. Once the failure to hold the convention by October, 1958, was brought to the attention of state insurance commissioners, whether by complaints from dissident unionists, by inquiries from members who were apprehensive about the validity of their policies, or by other means, the state officials in turn addressed inquiries to the top Brotherhood officers, and in some cases refused to renew the union's license as a fraternal insurance body. This was pressure that the union found difficult to resist, since protection of their insurance policies is important to large numbers of Brotherhood members.

The issue became acute on March 17, 1959, when Deputy Superintendent Ralph V. Thomen of the Ohio Department of Insurance sent identical letters to Kennedy and to Weil, reviewing past developments, and informing them that failure of the union to comply with the Ohio statute, by holding a convention and electing officers, before the renewal date of April 1, 1959, would mean that its license would not be renewed. These letters touched off an angry exchange between Weil, who was in the Cleveland office when they were received, and Kennedy, who at that moment was in Chicago. Weil informed Kennedy of the letters by telephone and said that he felt impelled to reply immediately; his reply to Thomen was a request for a reasonable length of time in which to comply, together with a recommendation that the Board of Directors be convened immediately to set a time and place for a convention.

On March 23 Kennedy sent a communication to all Grand Lodge officers, informing them of Thomen's letters and telling them that Brotherhood Attorney Ray T. Miller was confident that the union did not have to hold a convention every four years under the provision of the Ohio insurance law which exempted from this requirement fraternal organizations whose members were engaged in a single hazardous occupation. Assuring them that under no circumstances would anyone's insurance protection be jeopardized, he stated, in an obvious reference to Weil, that he did "not propose to stampede merely because someone, overwrought and nervous, hits the panic button." Weil in his reply retorted that "Perhaps someone is nervous, and showing signs of panic, but that someone is not the General Secretary and Treasurer."

On April 8 Titler, whose appeal from Kennedy's announcement of the postponement had been rejected, filed a suit in Ohio against the union, its Insurance Department, and the members of the Board of Directors. Reciting the constitutional provision on holding conventions, the circumstances of the referendum, and the refusal of the Ohio insurance superintendent to renew the union's license on April 1, 1959, Titler's suit asked the court for a writ of mandamus requiring the defendants to call a convention or to show cause why this should not be done. In response the union's attorneys cited the precedents of the 1934 and 1942 postponements, pointed out that the 1942 procedure had been approved by the 1946 convention, and argued that Section 4 of the constitution, providing that "The Grand Lodge shall meet quadrennially," was permissive, not mandatory.

On April 14 in a long letter to Kennedy, to which reference has already been made, Weil reviewed the struggle over the convention and the problem of compliance with the various fraternal insurance laws. Over a two-year period, he asserted, neither Kennedy nor the union's attorneys had conferred with him; as a result he had consulted an attorney of his own, whose opinion was that the Board of Directors had exceeded its authority in holding the referendum. Referring to "clever innuendoes" that he would be subjected to charges before the Executive Board unless he agreed to go along with the president, Weil, nevertheless, urged the early calling of a convention.

A new factor was injected into the controversy on April 17 when a New York City attorney, Francis X. McHugh, sent a letter to all local lodge chairmen of the Brotherhood. Stating that he represented several members of the union who were worried about their insurance, McHugh asserted that the Brotherhood's insurance license had been suspended in Ohio, and was endangered everywhere else. He urged the local lodge chairmen to demand an immediate convention as the only procedure to preserve the financial structure of the union and serve the peace of mind of the membership.[11]

A few days later Kennedy received a letter from Edward A. Stowell, Ohio Superintendent of Insurance, that was prompted by several inquiries from Brotherhood members concerning the status of their insurance benefits. Issuance of the renewal license, Stowell said, was being held in abeyance, following an agreement with the union's attorney, until the issue was finally determined by the courts or by the Department of Insurance. In the interim period, however, he wanted to assure members of the union that their insurance rights and policies were in no way impaired or jeopardized. Under the Ohio law, he pointed out, the union's license remained in effect until a new one was issued or specifically refused.

In May, Pennsylvania was added to the list of states with which the union's insurance program was in difficulty. On May 13 a letter from Insurance Commissioner Francis R. Smith advised Kennedy that the union's Insurance Department required a license to operate in Pennsylvania. On June 22, no application for a license having been filed, Smith served notice on the union's Insurance Department to cease doing business in the state.

In the meantime, a new group had made its appearance; from that time on it was to spearhead the struggle for a convention and to play a leading role in the opposition to Kennedy. This was the Committee of the Hundred, which was to remain anonymous throughout the entire fight. It consisted, according to its first circular, of 96 officers of the union, of whom 6 were general chairmen, 41 local chairmen, and 49 other local lodge officers. The first circular, dated May 25 and mailed from St. Louis on May 29 to all local lodges, criticized the referendum vote to postpone the convention as in violation of the constitution; pointed to the union's recent loss of 22,000 members and disputes with the various state insurance boards; quoted resolutions favoring a convention adopted by the Association of Local Grievance Committees, Chicago Switching District, and the Association of Local Committees, New York Harbor Switching District; reproduced recent Chicago and Cleveland news articles dealing with the convention issue; and urged locals to express their views on the subject.[12]

A week after the committee's circulars had been mailed from St. Louis, the Bi-State Association of Lodges, Illinois and Missouri, and the St. Louis Switching Association met in that city, and adopted a resolution supporting Kennedy's leadership and expressing resentment of the mailing of the anonymous circulars, that had been prepared elsewhere, in St. Louis, thereby casting suspicion upon the St. Louis membership of the union.[13]

In the weeks that followed other groups within the union adopted comparable resolutions, attacking the Committee of the Hundred and approving and supporting Kennedy's leadership. Many of the resolutions expressed regret for internal dissension at a time when the rail unions were under attack by the carriers on the featherbedding issue. Such resolutions included those adopted by the Greater Toledo Association, the New Orleans Switching Association, a joint meeting of the Texas State Association and the Dixie Boosters Association, the Board of Insurance, and the Board of Appeals.

The Board of Insurance and the Board of Appeals, in almost identical resolutions adopted on July 13, after condemning the anonymous, underground methods of the Committee of the Hundred as "calculated to injure and create dissension within our Brotherhood," expressed support of Kennedy and his leadership, and resolved that every effort be made to determine those responsible for the circulars and that proper action be taken against them under Brotherhood law.

Meanwhile, the Committee of the Hundred continued to issue its circulars to all local lodges at irregular intervals, mailed first from St. Louis and later from New York City. The second issue, dated June 26, regretted the necessity to remain anonymous, and asked readers to reflect "how serious the situation really is, when dedicated unionists, by reason of iron-fisted censorship, cannot sign their names to the TRUTH."

In the latter part of July further developments with opposite results to one another occurred under the insurance laws of Pennsylvania and Ohio. On July 21 Insurance Commissioner Smith of Pennsylvania, following up his earlier letter to the same effect to Kennedy, wrote to all lodge treasurers and field supervisors in that state directing them to stop any further insurance business in Pennsylvania, since the Brotherhood was not licensed in the state. The Pennsylvania law dealing with fraternal societies, the letter pointed out, required a meeting of the governing body and the election of officers to be held as often as once in every four calendar years. An accompanying press release quoted Commissioner Smith as saying that the law prohibited the collection of insurance premiums and assessments by unlicensed societies, but not the payment of claims or other benefits under insurance contracts.[14] The union's Insurance Department contested this decision in the courts, on the ground that the department came under the provision of the law exempting societies which limited their membership to a single hazardous occupation. On July 30 it filed a complaint in equity to that effect, seeking an injunction against Commissioner Smith.

In Ohio, where the same issue was already being litigated, a court decision upheld the union's interpretation. On July 27 the Court of Appeals of the Eighth Judicial District of Ohio denied the suit brought by Titler against the union, on the ground that the requirement for a convention in every four years did not apply, under Ohio law, to societies which limited their membership to any one hazardous occupation. Since railroading was a hazardous employment, the court held unanimously that the Brotherhood was not required to hold a convention.[15] Titler's appeal was pending when the 1960 convention was held. Testimony in the Pennsylvania hearing, held in October, showed, however, that the Brotherhood insured, not only railroaders, but also bus drivers, Grand Lodge employees, and children and grandchildren of members, regardless of their occupations. It was on these grounds that the court on January 26, 1960, while the convention was in session, dismissed the case,[16] thereby upholding Commissioner Smith's ruling.

On August 3 the Board of Directors revived a rule that had been in effect years earlier: that Grand Lodge officers could not leave the territory assigned to them unless instructed to do so by the president of the Brotherhood. The reason assigned was the issuance of anonymous circulars, calculated to create dissension within the Brotherhood, and making it necessary for each officer to remain in his home territory or office to protect the interests of the union.[17] The order had the effect of preventing General Secretary and Treasurer Weil (who had assumed leadership of the insurgent group and who was expected to oppose Kennedy for the presidency at the next convention) from traveling about the country and so promoting his candidacy unless he first obtained Kennedy's permission.

Further pressure for a convention was added by the Codes of Ethical Practices of the AFL-CIO, with which the Trainmen had affiliated in 1957, and by the Labor-Management Reporting and Disclosure Act of 1959. Point 4 of the Code on Union Democratic Processes called on national unions to hold regular conventions at stated intervals of not more than four years. The codes, though not legally binding, had some impact in that violating unions might be subject to inquiry from the Committee on Ethical Practices of the AFL-CIO. On September 1 a group of Brotherhood members wrote anonymously to President George Meany of the Federation, reciting some of the developments that have been outlined here, emphasizing the need for a convention, and asking Meany to point out to Kennedy and his associates that their actions had created discontent and distrust among members of the union. Copies of the letter were sent to the Ethical Practices Committee of the AFL-CIO, to Grand Lodge officers, to general chairmen, and to all lodges.[18]

The other pressure was more compelling. The new federal labor law, approved September 14, 1959, required national unions to elect officers every five years or less. Whereas unionism and collective bargaining on the railroads had been exempted from earlier general labor relations enactments on the ground that this industry was covered by its own legislation, in this instance, railroad unions were subject to the law along with others. In the opinion of a number of labor lawyers, including the general counsel of the Trainmen, the five-year period might be held to run retroactively, and it was just five years since the last convention of the Brotherhood had been held. The union could not afford to take a chance on a ruling that it was not in compliance with the law. By the time that Secretary of Labor James P. Mitchell ruled that the five-year period was not to be applied retroactively, the union's convention was already in session.

The Call for a Special Convention

On October 3 Kennedy announced that he was calling a special convention in order to amend the constitution to conform to the new federal labor law and to elect Grand Lodge officers. The new law, it was pointed out, required the election of international officers not less often than once every five years, and the five-year period ended in 1959. Numerous other changes, Kennedy stated, would be required to conform to the new federal legislation. Delegates to the 1954 convention were to attend the special convention, with the lodges electing new delegates or alternate delegates where vacancies existed. Under the Brotherhood's constitution, the president possesses the authority to call a special convention, whereas a regular convention can be called only by the Board of Directors; it was to avoid this delay in the calling of the convention, Kennedy has asserted, that he called a special rather than a regular convention.

Once the call for the special convention was issued, the Committee of the Hundred intensified its efforts, issuing five new circulars plus a reissue of an old one in the last three months of the year, as compared with only three in the preceding four and a half months. Its objective now was to persuade the delegates, once they assembled, to transform the meeting into a regular convention. As a special convention, the delegates could act only on matters specified by the president; but the delegates were the Grand Lodge, the Committee pointed out, with supreme authority over the Brotherhood's affairs. The Committee's circulars attacked the quality of the Brotherhood's present leadership, and urged the delegates to place a sixty-five-year limit on the age of officers.

This was the situation, then, when approximately 1,100 delegates assembled in Cleveland for the convention called for January 4, 1960. A number of the developments at that convention will be detailed in a later chapter dealing with Brotherhood conventions. Before that topic is taken up, however, attention will be paid to Grand Lodge officers other than the president, and also to staff officials.

6

The Other Grand Lodge Offices

Besides the president, Grand Lodge officers include an assistant to the president, fifteen vice presidents, eight alternate vice presidents, a general secretary and treasurer, an assistant general secretary and treasurer, a national legislative representative, an alternate national legislative representative, a Canadian legislative representative, an alternate Canadian legislative representative, and five boards—a Board of Directors, an Individual Reserve Board, a Board of Trustees and Insurance, an Executive Board, and a Board of Appeals. There is also an alternate each to the Board of Trustees and Insurance and to the Executive Board, and four alternates to the Board of Appeals. Whereas the Board of Directors and the Individual Reserve Board are made up of ex officio members, the members of the other three boards are elected specifically to those posts. The large number of boards in the Trainmen helps to keep power diffused, as contrasted with the more typical situation in which a single general executive board performs a variety of functions.

The positions of alternates to the various offices and boards were created by the 1960 convention, which also established a sliding scale of eligibility, based on age, for Grand Lodge officers.

Since the sliding scale assured the retirement of a number of Grand Lodge officers and board members before the next convention met, the delegates preferred to designate those who would succeed to their positions rather than to leave the filling of the vacancies, as in the past, in the hands of the Board of Directors.

As of November 1, 1959, the scale of pay for these offices was $20,079.00 each for the assistant president, the general secretary and treasurer, and the national legislative representative; $15,-600.00 for each of the vice presidents; $15,534.00 for each of the trustees; $14,319.00 for the assistant general secretary and treasurer; and $34.40 daily for members of the Board of Appeals and the Executive Board. Since then Grand Lodge salaries, except for officers, have been raised moderately (under 4 per cent) in line with the union's policy of matching, for its officers and staff, the percentage increases obtained for its members in national wage movements. The officers received a $25.00 per month increase.

The assistant to the president has no prescribed constitutional duties, other than to help the president as presiding officer when conventions are in session, and to perform such other duties as the president may assign to him. The president normally assigns the assistant to the president to some of the most important national activities that should be handled by a senior officer, but that require more time and detailed attention than the president himself can give. When the Brotherhood embarks upon a national wage or rules movement, the assistant to the president is often appointed to chair the committee, which usually includes several vice presidents and a number of representative general chairmen from the various portions of the country. The assistant to the president is also given a number of grievance committee assignments, particularly in the area in which he was active before becoming a national officer. He may also be assigned by the president to end unauthorized strikes, investigate cases of rival union activity among the membership, look into serious problems within a lodge, organize new lodges, or represent the union at meetings of various types.

Until 1960, following the death, resignation, or removal of the president, the assistant to the president had the duty of convening the Board of Directors to elect a successor, in the meantime performing the duties of the president. Because of the importance of his office and of the widespread contacts it afforded, the assistant to the president was a logical choice for the presidency, as was the general secretary and treasurer. In 1960 the constitution was changed to provide for the automatic succession to the presidency, in the event of a vacancy, of the assistant to the president.

The general secretary and treasurer is in a stronger position, in an important sense, since his duties with regard to the receipt and custody of funds, the safeguarding of important papers, and the preparation of reports are defined in the constitution, without any requirement that he report to the president or work under the latter's direction. The duties of the general secretary and treasurer keep him in necessary and frequent communication with the lodges, a political asset of no mean importance. His communications, however, relate to financial matters, and in no sense permit him to invade the areas over which authority is reserved to the president. Though the general secretary and treasurer may communicate freely with lodges within a narrow range of subject matter, he does not enjoy the publicity and prestige advantage, often available to the assistant to the president, of representing the union in national wage or rules movements. Both Whitney and Kennedy successfully achieved the presidency from the vantage point of the general secretary and treasurer's office, though both had earlier held vice presidencies; and in the most recent presidential race Weil, who until then had been general secretary and treasurer, unsuccessfully sought the presidency. The consistency with which the general secretary and treasurer's post has been used as a springboard for the presidency suggests that its independence from the president, along with its communications facilities with the lodges, constitute distinct political assets.

The Vice Presidents

All of the fifteen vice presidents are elected by the convention at large, though a common understanding exists that Canada, the various regions within the United States, and groups with specialized problems will all receive representation within the vice presidential group. This practice serves both to provide an avenue of recognition to each group of officers, and to assure that the higher ranks of the Brotherhood will possess officers competent to deal with any type of specialized problems. By common consent two of the vice presidencies are reserved for the Canadian membership. While no comparable understanding exists with regard to the distribution of the remaining thirteen vice presidencies, representation is always given to each of the three geographic areas, the East, the West, and the South, into which the United States traditionally has been divided for railroading purposes. A vice president from one of these areas, running for re-election, would normally be opposed only by candidates from the same region, though anyone is free to run. Usually there is at least one vice president from the short line roads, some of which are operated by steel companies, which have their own peculiar set of problems. Regardless of the area from which a vice president comes, he may be assigned duties anywhere within the Brotherhood's jurisdiction at the discretion of the president.

When alternate vice presidencies were established in 1960, a requirement was written into the constitution that two each should be chosen from the three regions of the United States, one from Canada, and one from the bus membership. Except for the Canadian officer, the alternates are advanced to vice presidencies in the order of their respective majorities, without regard to the jurisdiction represented by the former officer whose vacancy is being filled.

Though the delegates are aware of regional considerations in the election of the vice presidents, the requirement that each of the fifteen receive a majority vote of the convention delegates tends to weaken sectional ties. If the president could control the combination of votes that elected him, every vice president would be dependent for election upon the president's support. In practice the voting lines fluctuate to a substantial degree, particularly after the elections to the most important offices have been concluded. In practice supporters of the president who are ambitious to become vice presidents seek his endorsement and usually will not make the race if denied his support. Upon occasion he will state that each of two or more candidates is acceptable to him, in which case all will run, allowing their popularity with the delegates to determine the issue. Antiadministration or independent candidates, needless to say, would neither seek nor get the president's support, though they may seek the approval of the president's leading rival, if there is one; or, if they are candidates for different offices, they may seek to combine their voting strength. If vice presidents were elected by regional conventions, or by the delegates to the convention who come from a particular region, a vice president's ties to the area he serves would likely be strengthened, and his dependence upon the president's support correspondingly reduced.

Though each region is reasonably assured of representation in the ranks of vice presidents, the particular numbered vice presidencies (the position in the seniority sequence) are not assigned by regions. As vacancies occur by death, resignation, or retirement, all the vice presidents below the opening move up a notch, and the newly elevated vice president becomes the fifteenth in order. The order is important for reasons other than prestige, since the four senior vice presidents from the United States, and also the senior Canadian vice president, serve on the Brotherhood's Board of Directors. Though any vice president is free at any convention to run for a vice presidency higher on the list, such behavior is frowned upon among the seniority-conscious members of the Brotherhood. So ingrained is this feeling for seniority that at the 1954 convention, for example, a motion was adopted, just prior to the election of the vice presidents, "that any new candidate for the office of vice president, if elected, follow those who are now holding office. This is in line with the railroad man's observance of seniority rights, and this is also in line with action taken in previous conventions." C. J. McClain, who had been tenth vice president prior to the 1954 convention, was defeated that year for re-election to his old position, but elected to the fourteenth vice presidency. As a result of the motion referred to above, the official *Directory,* when published, showed McClain in the twelfth position, and Charles Luna, who had been elected the tenth vice president, as the thirteenth instead.[1]

The vice presidents are assigned by the president to work in particular territories, the boundaries of which he determines and can change at any time. This power readily becomes one of political control, since the president may assign a vice president whom he distrusts to a small and unpromising territory, far removed from the latter's sources of political strength; in this he runs the risk, of course, that a capable and personable vice president may take advantage of the assignment to build a new circle of friends to add to those he has already made in his former territory. This is what happened, in fact, during Whitney's period as vice president, when his assignment was changed by Lee. In his assigned territory a vice president can attend meetings of lodges as he chooses. If he leaves his territory without authority of the president he is not paid salary, per diem, or expenses; unless he is willing to forego these payments, therefore, he may attend lodges in other areas only if he is sent into such area by the president, as on a grievance assignment, and if one of the lodges there happens to be meeting at that time.

Within his assigned territory the vice president visits lodges, serves as an avenue of communication between the local groups and the national organization, offers advice on internal problems as well as on grievance handling, and exercises a general supervision over the interests of the Brotherhood. He cannot inject himself into a situation, however, but must wait to be assigned by the president of the Brotherhood. Such assignments may deal with grievance or collective bargaining problems, in which a vice president is often helpful because he brings the prestige of the Grand Lodge to the negotiations; or the president may assign him to investigate disagreements within a lodge, complaints of members about the handling of their affairs, controversies over lodge finances, protests over the conduct of lodge elections, or charges of irregularities of any sort. A vice president may also be assigned to investigate the setting up of a new lodge or the closing of an old one, or to look after Brotherhood interests in a representation election.

In all such assignments the vice president makes a report with recommendations to the president, who concurs in the recommendations in almost all cases. The president, however, is not bound to assign a problem to a vice president simply because it arises within his geographic area; often the president assigns such problems to a deputy president instead, either because he thinks the deputy president better qualified to deal with the particular assignment, or because the volume of work is too great for the vice president to handle.

The president may assign a vice president to a variety of other tasks as well. If a state legislative representative wants help in an important legislative battle, as over a full crew law, a vice president may be assigned to assist. He may also serve, by appointment of the president, on a national wage-rules committee either in the United States or Canada, depending on his nationality; if he is a Canadian vice president, he may chair the Brotherhood committee in that country. Or a vice president may be appointed to an important staff position, such as the head of the Field Service Department, to which he brings the prestige of his Grand Lodge office. He may also be asked to represent the president at social functions within his area, or to act for the president on ceremonial occasions, such as the presentation of long-service membership pins.

The National Legislative Representative

The Brotherhood's key official in the effort to influence federal legislation is its national legislative representative. This officer does not determine policy. In a very broad sense, policy is a function of the convention, and between the time that conventions are held, it is a function of the president—so long as he operates within the limits, usually quite broad, of convention authorization. But the national legislative representative, as the Brotherhood representative in closest touch with the Congressional scene, is in the best position to recommend the precise legislative policy most likely to be successful in view of shifting opinions and pressures in Washington. The president of the Brotherhood, in turn, is likely to rely to a very great extent upon the informed judgment of the national legislative representative. Typically, the candidates for this post have had a background of long and successful experience as state legislative representatives.

After a legislative objective is decided upon, an attorney for the Brotherhood may draft a bill, which a friendly member of Congress then introduces. The national legislative representative may work with the chairman of the committee to which the bill is assigned to get hearings scheduled, at which the president of the Brotherhood or the national legislative representative may present the Brotherhood's position. More often, however, the Railway Labor Executives' Association designates one of its members to serve as spokesman for all the rail unions. If grass-roots pressure is desired, word to that effect is sent to the state legislative representatives, who in turn contact their local legislative representatives. Similarly, the issue is publicized in *Trainman News* and also in *Labor,* the organ of all the railroad brotherhoods, with both papers asking for local lodge resolutions and for letters from members to their respective Congressmen. In important cases state legislative representatives may be called to Washington to contact senators and representatives from their states.

Once a bill is pending in Congress, decisions often have to be made as to whether suggested modifications should be accepted. If the modifications are minor, the national legislative representative uses his own judgment, based upon his assessment of the legislative situation; or, if the RLEA is working for the measure, the national legislative representative meets with his counterparts in the other rail unions so that a joint decision may be made. Important changes, however, would not be accepted without the concurrence of the president of the Brotherhood, and major matters would wait for the monthly meetings of the RLEA, which the president of the Brotherhood usually attends. If he is unable to come, he usually authorizes the national legislative representative to attend in his place.

Members of the Brotherhood who are anxious for particular legislative gains are apt to communicate with the national legislative representative, who is thus kept in close touch with rank-and-file sentiments as well as with the pronouncements of official bodies of the union. Not all the improvements desired by the membership can be translated into a legislative program, however; sometimes proposals are not practicable, sometimes they are too expensive, and sometimes they involve conflicting interests within the ranks of the Brotherhood. Junior members, for example, may urge legislation to establish a low compulsory retirement age, to which senior members may be strongly opposed. In any event, no action could be taken on such a proposal without considering the impact both on premiums and on benefits under the retirement legislation. Nevertheless, the national legislative representative would keep the president informed if a large volume of mail came to him on this or on any other subject.

Getting a measure on the statute books does not end the duties of the national legislative representative with regard to it, for the law must then be policed. As violations of federal law occur, members report the matter to their local legislative representatives, who in turn forward the reports to the national legislative representative. Or the complaints may go through the hands of the state legislative representative or through the president's office before being transmitted to the national legislative representative. If he wishes, the local legislative representative may report the violation directly to the Interstate Commerce Commission, though it is far more efficient to act through the national legislative representative, who knows the personnel and the procedures of the Commission and who may get reports of a number of violations on the same railroad and be in a position to coordinate the Brotherhood's efforts. By way of illustration of this enforcement process, a brakeman may notice that a grab iron has been mashed against the side of a car, creating a safety hazard in violation of the Safety Appliance Act. The brakeman would report the number of the car to his local legislative representative, along with an account of the car's movement in interstate commerce. In due time a complaint would be filed by the national legislative representative with the Interstate Commerce Commission; the ICC, following its investigation, would learn whether the car had been repaired, and would so report to the Brotherhood.

The national legislative representative also keeps a watch on the filing of applications with the Interstate Commerce Commission for abandonments or consolidations of service or mergers of railroads, any of which, if approved, would likely reduce the volume of employment available to Brotherhood members. The national legislative representative, besides keeping the president of the Brotherhood informed of all such developments, notifies the general chairmen of the roads involved and also the affected state legislative representatives. If the membership of the union would be affected adversely by the proposed change, the local chairmen or the general chairman concerned would ask the president of the Brotherhood to file a protest. Such protests are usually filed through the Railway Labor Executives' Association.

Though the railroads and the railroad brotherhoods typically are ranged on opposite sides of legislative battles, there are a number of issues on which their interests are similar. Thus the unions are as interested as are their employers in measures that would make their industry more competitive, and better able to hold and attract business. Proposals for tax relief or for government loans for the railroads often find the national legislative representative and the lobbyists for the railroads cooperating, as they do in conflicts between the railroads and the trucking industry over rates and subsidies, or in opposition to the construction of pipelines that would divert traffic from the rails. When the unions help to pass some measure that the railroads want, they may exact a price for their cooperation, as by agreement upon a provision safeguarding some threatened jobs or conferring some additional benefit upon railroad employees. In other cases the plight of the roads may be so desperate that assurance of continued operation is reward enough to obtain the full cooperation of the Brotherhood in support of the management program.

The national legislative representative in the United States has his counterpart in the Canadian legislative representative, who deals with the Dominion government centered in Ottawa. Differences in their functions and methods of operation reflect differences in Canadian tradition, in the allocation of authority between federal and provincial government, and in the parliamentary system of government as opposed to that prevailing in the United States. Another major difference is that the Canadian National Railways, one of the two principal systems operating in Canada, is owned by the government, and is plagued by constantly recurring deficits. The Canadian National, therefore, is in a weaker position to resist political pressure than are the privately owned roads, either in the United States or in Canada.

The Brotherhood's legislative policy in Canada is formulated by the Canadian Legislative Board, which consists of the ten provincial chairmen. They are influenced, in turn, by membership sentiment, which is channeled to them through the local legislative representatives. As in the United States, all proposed legislation must be approved by the president of the Brotherhood, though in practice the differences between the two countries makes it extremely unlikely that the president would overrule the judgment of the Canadian officers of the union. Policy is carried out by the Canadian legislative representative who, as in the United States, seeks both to effect the passage of favorable legislation and to see to its interpretation and enforcement.

In Canada the Brotherhood maintains friendly relations with

both major parties, and is equally influential with them in the matters that concern members of the union most closely. Its legislative success depends more on the person named Minister of Transport in the government than on any other single factor. On matters of safety, and also on proposed railroad abandonments, the Canadian legislative representative works with the Board of Transport Commissioners. The Brotherhood is less active in a partisan political sense than in the United States, however. It endorses neither party nor candidates, leaving such activities to the judgment of the individual members.

The Board of Directors

The Board of Directors is perhaps the most important of the five boards that are part of the Grand Lodge structure, because of the combination of policy-making and judicial functions that it performs. While the policy-making powers are not spelled out clearly in the constitution, their scope will be apparent from the actions that the Board of Directors has taken as issues have arisen. It was the Board of Directors that decided in 1956 to hold a referendum vote on postponing the convention, and that in the following year recommended to the president, the general secretary and treasurer, and the Board of Trustees that a monthly assessment of twenty-five cents be levied to build up a convention fund. It was the Board of Directors, similarly, that resolved in the summer of 1959 that Grand Lodge officers who left their assigned territories without specific authorization by the president would not be paid salary, per diem, or other expenses. In 1955 the Board of Directors authorized Kennedy to confer with George Meany of the AFL and Walter Reuther of the CIO, looking toward the affiliation of the Trainmen with the merged labor federation; and two years later the Board heard and approved Kennedy's reports on the successful completion of affiliation negotiations with the AFL-CIO and also on the Trainmen's affiliation with the Canadian Labour Congress.

The Board has also considered the holding of referenda on such questions as limiting the length of conventions and changing the union's strike benefit plan, and it has authorized and fixed the amounts of expense allotments to state legislative representatives. The constitution empowers the Board of Directors to appoint the convention committees on the constitution and on the reports of Grand Lodge officers. In the event of disagreement between the president and the national or the Canadian legislative representative on legislative policy, the Board of Directors is authorized to settle the matter.

Until 1960 the Board also had the very important power of filling vacancies in the ranks of Grand Lodge officers caused by death, resignation, or removal. With the creation of a number of alternate Grand Lodge posts that year, the power of the Board with regard to vacancies was limited to the filling of temporary vacancies caused by illness or absence, and appointments to fill vacancies for which no alternates had been elected.

The Board of Directors also shares appellate jurisdiction with the Board of Appeals, the former board hearing appeals from decisions of the president of the Brotherhood where a question of Brotherhood law is involved and the latter hearing appeals involving the merits of grievances or matters of policy in collective bargaining or legislative affairs. The types of cases involving the interpretation or application of Brotherhood law are varied. They may involve lodge actions in not accepting or in closing out grievances, lodge actions relating to seniority, rulings by the lodge president, eligibility to run for office, irregularities in elections, removals from office, expulsions by lodges, reductions of salary of lodge or general committee officers, disputes between lodges over jurisdiction, or changes negotiated by the lodge in the agreement.

Appeals may also relate to actions taken by general chairmen or general committees on claims or other grievances, on the rights of men in different seniority districts to disputed types of work, or on such controversial issues as compulsory retirement. Or appeals may be based on the negotiation of a change in an agreement by a vice president or deputy president; or on the action of the president of the Brotherhood removing men from subordinate lodge office, revising the jurisdiction of lodges, settling disputes between general committees over rights to disputed work, or directing committee members to sign revised agreements that had been negotiated. However the issue arises, it goes to the president of the Brotherhood before it can come before the Board of Directors, so that in form it is always an appeal from a decision of the president. Decisions of the Board of Directors, which handles twenty to thirty appeals cases in a typical year, may be appealed in turn to the convention.

The division of authority in appeals cases between the Board of Directors and the Board of Appeals is not always a very clear one. Section 71 of the constitution, dealing with that document's interpretation, provides for initial decision by the president, for appeal to or intervention by the Board of Directors, and finally for appeal to the convention, without any jurisdiction to the Board of Appeals. Under Section 139, however, dealing with trials, removals from office, lodge decisions, or legislative Board actions, the president's decision is to be appealed first to the Board of Directors and then to the Board of Appeals, except that the latter tribunal has no jurisdiction over cases involving the application of Brotherhood law. Appeals, therefore, go from the president to the Board of Directors when the issue is one of union law, and to the Board of Appeals if the merits of a grievance or of a collective bargaining or legislative policy are involved. In certain types of cases, such as disciplinary actions, appeals go first to the Board of Directors and then to the Board of Appeals.

The Board of Directors is composed of the president, the assistant to the president, the four senior United States vice presidents, the senior Canadian vice president, the general secretary and treasurer, the national legislative representative, the Canadian legislative representative, and the chairman of the Board of Trustees and Insurance. The president does not participate in cases involving appeals from his decision, the assistant to the president serving as presiding officer in such cases. Due process is observed throughout, with letters to all parties concerned asking for reports on the issue and with an opportunity for interested parties to appear in person. Often the members of the board seek to preserve the appearance of unity—however sharply they may disagree among themselves—to avoid weakening the union's position in the eyes of management.

How freely the Board of Directors is likely to reverse a president upon an issue about which he feels strongly depends upon the relations between them and the personalities involved. During a large part of Whitney's tenure in office, the majority of the Board—political opponents of his—blocked him on a large number of issues. The fact that the vice presidents who serve on the

Board are senior officers with long experience in Brotherhood affairs strengthens their independence, as does the fact that Board voting is by secret ballot. On the other hand, the composition of the Board places its members in a weak position to serve as a check upon decisions by the president, since the five vice presidents are subject to the president's authority in the way that has been described, and since the assistant to the president and the national legislative representative likewise work under his direction to a substantial degree. Only the general secretary and treasurer and the chairman of the trustees are in relatively independent positions.

Nor can it be expected that a board so constituted can be unaware of political considerations that impinge upon its judicial functions. For example, when Kennedy issued his circular in October, 1959, calling a special convention of the Brotherhood to meet on the following January 4, he ruled that the 1954 delegates would attend. Only if both the regular and the alternate delegates elected in 1953 had died, retired, or become disqualified for other reasons would a lodge be represented by someone elected more recently. Lodge 909 appealed to the Board of Directors that portion of Kennedy's circular dealing with the use of the 1954 delegates, on the ground that this action violated rights acquired by the membership under the Labor-Management Reporting and Disclosure Act of 1959, and arguing also that the constitution of the Brotherhood had been violated by this ruling. The issue was considered on January 2, 1960, two days before the convention opened, by a Board of Directors which included the two prospective rival candidates for the presidency, along with many of the chief supporters of one of them. One could hardly expect the thinking of such a board, under such circumstances, to be unaffected by political considerations.[2]

While this is an extreme case, the composition of the Board makes it likely that political considerations will influence the judicial process in certain types of cases. All members serve on the Board by virtue of their election to posts that are essentially administrative in nature, and all who wish to be continued in the same or another Grand Lodge position must take their chances in the election process at the following convention. While the bulk of the appeals that the Board considers are non-political in nature, in cases with political aspects members of the Board may be aware that their decision may have an impact on their own political fortunes. When factional lines are tightly drawn, indeed, almost any case may involve political considerations, since the appellant is likely to be sympathetic to one of the political groupings. Only when there is an independent judiciary, chosen for judicial qualities and given security of position, can one reasonably expect political considerations to be minimized, if not eliminated from consideration.

Until the 1960 convention created the system of alternates, the Board of Directors was empowered to fill vacancies in the list of Grand Lodge offices. In view of the large number of officers and members of the various boards, and also the advanced age of many of the officers, this was a power of considerable importance, particularly since the seniority-conscious delegates were likely to return officers to their positions. Often the Board of Directors appointed a member of one of the boards to a vice presidency when such a position was open, or promoted one from a part-time membership, as on the Executive Board, to a full-time position with the Board of Appeals or the Trustees. Such a procedure permitted two promotions as the result of a single vacancy.

Critics of this system of filling vacancies argued that too much power was thus concentrated in the hands of a small group of men, and that it was more democratic to permit the convention to designate the men who were to be promoted. Defenders of the old system suggested that the Board of Directors, knowing each candidate personally, could judge which one was best qualified to fill a particular opening, whereas the convention might select a nominee who, though popular with the delegates, lacked qualifications for the office. The same considerations, it should be noted, could be urged against any choice by the convention, for regular officers as for alternates.

When a vacancy occurs, a large number of names may be before the Board of Directors, since any member of the Brotherhood may get a friend to nominate him, without any requirement that he obtain endorsement by his lodge, and since any member of the board is free to suggest names. Votes on all candidates are by secret ballot, and members of the board are free to vote their convictions. Often there is a split vote, and in some cases two or more ballots have been required before a nominee received the required majority vote of the members of the board. Yet a strong president may be able to secure support for candidates he favors, so long as these candidates are able and competent men, in view of the fact that many of the board members work under the president's direction and some may be dependent upon his influence for re-election.[3] In practice the president often submits the names of two candidates who are acceptable to him, permitting the board a free choice between them.

The Board of Trustees and Insurance

The Board of Trustees and Insurance is composed of three members, one of whom must be a Canadian, who devote their full time to the financial affairs of the Brotherhood. They examine vouchers submitted in connection with expenditures to make sure that the expenditure is properly authorized under Brotherhood rules. Since the funds of general committees and of state legislative boards are maintained at the Grand Lodge headquarters, the trustees review these expenditures as well as those of Grand Lodge funds. If the clerks in the office of the general secretary and treasurer are in doubt as to the validity of particular expenditures, they may consult the trustees before issuing checks. In the case of an honest mistake by some officer, who obtains funds improperly or spends money in violation of the union's regulations, the trustees would see that restitution is made. If they believe that the officer is deliberately violating the constitution, however, they would file charges against him. Cases of this sort have occurred in the past, though not in recent years. Though the volume of accident and health claims under Brotherhood insurance policies is too large for a full audit, the trustees conduct spot checks from time to time. Once a year they have a complete audit of the union's books made by a firm of certified public accountants. The trustees also see that all officers are properly bonded, and they have the responsibility, in conjunction with the president and the general secretary and treasurer, of investing the insurance funds of the union, now totaling almost $50,000,000.00.

Extraordinary expenses, those not covered by provisions in the constitution, require the approval of the president, the general secretary and treasurer, and the trustees. Such an expenditure, for example, would be one to improve a building owned by the union. Or a general committee, finding its funds running low, might ask the president for help, and he might recommend to the trustees that a loan be made from the Brotherhood's general funds. Similarly, the president and the general secretary and treasurer, in conjunction with the trustees, have the power to levy special assessments, such as for a convention fund, and they are also empowered to assess the membership, not to exceed two dollars per member in any one month, to build up the union's protective and strike funds.

Another power, vested in the trustees by constitutional provision, is to approve the compensation of office employees at Grand Lodge headquarters in cases where no specific sum is named by convention action. Under this provision the trustees traditionally have asserted that their approval was needed before the president could create any additional positions or increase the salaries paid to existing employees. This power became the subject of dispute shortly after the 1954 convention, when Kennedy made several personnel reclassifications and salary adjustments, in accordance with a resolution adopted by the convention, without obtaining the approval of the trustees. The trustees appealed the president's action to the Board of Directors, which denied the appeal. In April, 1955, the trustees unanimously filed an appeal for certification to the following convention.

By the time the convention met, however, one of the three trustees had died and another had retired, and the two new trustees voted on the eve of the convention to withdraw the appeal. The remaining old trustee carried his appeal to the convention, arguing on the procedural issue that the new trustees, not having been appellants, could not properly withdraw the appeal; and on the substantive issue that a convention resolution could not set aside the provisions of the constitution. The convention, however, denied his appeal by a vote of 621 to 473. The trustee who presented the appeal, C. M. Wilkinson, was a leader of the insurgent group at the convention, and had been elected chairman of the Committee of the Whole, which revises the constitution, over an administration candidate. The convention decision limited the powers of the trustees over the salaries of Grand Lodge employees only to a moderate degree, it should be noted, since in this case the president acted under a convention mandate.[4]

The position of trustee is considered a highly desirable one, by comparison with any Grand Lodge post below the level of the top four offices. Though the trustee is paid slightly less than a vice president, he has the advantage of remaining at home, whereas a vice president must be traveling most of the time. Often a trustee prefers to remain in that post, even though a vice presidency, should one be available, would be considered a promotion. In other cases, however, the trustee may prefer a vice presidential post.

In 1960 the Board of Trustees was combined with the Board of Insurance, which until then had been a board of seven members who met semi-annually to consider insurance claims which had been appealed following disapproval or rejection by the Individual Reserve Board. The Board of Insurance had a limited volume of work, which could be added to the duties of the trustees, who were full-time, salaried officers, without burden to them, and at a saving to the Brotherhood. There was even an advantage to claimants, in that their appeals could be heard promptly, without waiting until the Board of Insurance assembled for its semi-annual meeting. Particularly where a man was disabled, it was important that his appeal be heard promptly. Whereas in earlier years the Board of Insurance had had a longer docket of appeals to consider, its case load had dwindled in the more recent period, because the policy of the Insurance Department was to approve and pay promptly all claims that seemed legitimate.

The functions of the Individual Reserve Board, which consists of the president, the assistant to the president, and the general secretary and treasurer, are limited to the insurance side of the Brotherhood's activities. The Board has the power to issue additional classes of insurance, to adopt regulations for the conduct of the insurance business, and to consider claims that have been disapproved by the general secretary and treasurer and referred to it by him or by a member of the Insurance Department. Appeals from the Individual Reserve Board are heard by the Board of Trustees and Insurance, whose decision is final.

The Executive Board

The Executive Board, a body of five, has as its sole function the hearing of charges filed against Grand Lodge officers. The constitution makes the usual provision for due process in such cases, and empowers the Executive Board, should it find the accused guilty, to censure or suspend him or remove him from office. An officer who is suspended or removed has the right to appeal to the next convention, which by majority vote may reverse a decision of the Executive Board. Members of the Board are paid on a per diem basis when engaged in their Grand Lodge duties. They have had no such duties since 1951, when the last hearing was held on charges filed against a Grand Lodge officer. Kennedy has filed no such charges since he became president in 1949.

However, Whitney, who was impatient of opposition, kept the Executive Board busy with charges against officers who challenged his will. The years 1941 and 1942 were particularly busy ones for the Executive Board, as an earlier chapter has showed, with the national legislative representative, a vice president, and four of the seven members of the Board of Appeals removed by the Executive Board on charges filed by Whitney. In 1947 the Executive Board, again acting on charges filed by Whitney, removed Baumberger and Bassett, two of the three trustees, in a case that resulted in constitutional changes. Until 1950 a two-thirds convention vote was required to reverse a decision of the Executive Board, a percentage that Baumberger and Bassett failed to get, although more than a majority of the delegates supported their appeal. The convention thereupon amended the constitution to permit a majority of the delegates to reverse the Executive Board.

Another constitutional change that resulted from the Baumberger-Bassett case was the insertion in the constitution of a clause prohibiting members of the Executive Board from representing the Brotherhood in any other capacity while serving on that board. Whitney had regularly given the members of the Executive Board assignments as deputy presidents or organizers, so that failure to support his charges in cases in which he felt strongly might involve risking the loss of such employment with the Grand Lodge. This is not to suggest that board members found evidence of wrong-doing where there was none, but rather that they removed men from office on evidence of petty violations, or for mere errors of judgment. The constitutional change adopted in 1950, forbidding other Grand Lodge appointments to Executive Board members, therefore represented a notable step in the direction of democratic controls. Yet the problem is not entirely solved, since members of the Executive Board may be ambitious for election to a full-time position with the Grand Lodge, and eager to obtain the president's support. Whether members of the Executive Board have been influenced by the desires of the president has been a function of their integrity and their ambition.

Though Kennedy has never filed charges against another Grand Lodge officer, and hence has had no occasion to seek to influence Executive Board decisions, he has sought to determine the choice of its chairman. Under the constitution the board is empowered to elect its own chairman. When the chairmanship was vacant in 1956 and again in 1958, however, Kennedy sent wires to the members of the board, asking them to confirm by return wire his choice for the chairmanship of the board; in one case Kennedy's candidate had just been named to the Executive Board by the Board of Directors, and in the other instance Kennedy predicted that his candidate would be named the following day.[5] In both cases the members of the board acceded to Kennedy's wishes. Their favorable votes might have been based upon their belief that the candidates proposed by the president for the chairmanship were best qualified to serve in that capacity, or they might have considered the chairmanship of little consequence, or they might have been unwilling to oppose the president's wishes. If the last-named consideration existed it would suggest that the board, while in a stronger position in relation to the president than was true in the Whitney period, has yet to achieve the independence that will permit it to function properly as an impartial judicial agency in a charged political atmosphere.

The Board of Appeals

There are two avenues by which issues are raised with the Board of Appeals. In one type of case a member or a lodge challenges the merits of an action taken by a general committee, either in disposing of a grievance or in negotiating changes in the agreement with the carrier. The other type of case originates in a subordinate lodge or with a legislative board; an officer or member who thinks that an injustice has been done him in a trial or a removal from office, or by a decision of his lodge or an action of a legislative board, may appeal to the president of the Brotherhood, whose decision in turn may be appealed to the Board of Directors and then to the Board of Appeals. If a question of Brotherhood law is concerned, however, the Board of Appeals has no jurisdiction, the line of appeal there being from the president to the Board of Directors, and then to the convention. Where the Board of Appeals has jurisdiction its decision is final. Whereas any decision by the Board of Directors may be appealed to the following convention, this is not the case with decisions by the Board of Appeals. A case that has been decided by the latter board requires the assent of two-thirds of the delegates before it may be brought before the convention.

The volume of business handled by the Board is substantial, ranging from about fifty to one hundred or more cases each year. Most of these appeals are filed by individual members or subordinate lodges, questioning the wisdom or justice of actions taken by a general committee or subgeneral committee with regard to grievances or changes in the agreement. A member or a lodge may complain that a claim was withdrawn or compromised by the committee when it should have been prosecuted to the fullest extent, or the full relief asked for obtained; thus a man who has been disciplined by the carrier may object because his case was withdrawn, or because it was settled for reinstatement to the service when, in his view, back pay should also have been obtained. Other cases may involve efforts of men to get higher places on their seniority rosters. Time claims raised on appeal may be of any category filed on the railroad; they may involve requests for pay for work done outside one's craft jurisdiction or seniority district, or they may be filed by men who were not called to work when some of their normal duties were performed by workmen of other crafts, or by men of the same craft who stood lower on the seniority roster. Other claims may be based on alleged crossing of jurisdictional boundaries between the work of roadmen and yardmen, between roadmen of adjoining seniority districts, or between switchmen and some other group of workers, such as carmen or mechanical department employees.

Other categories of cases may involve disputes between two groups of union members over the division of work. Thus two adjoining road districts may quarrel over work equities or inter-divisional runs, or two general committees may be unable to agree on the division of work on a joint facility. In the latter type of case the appeal typically is from the decision of the president of the Brotherhood, concurring in the recommendation for settlement of the issue made by a Grand Lodge officer sent in to investigate the dispute. Still another procedure is followed when the president of the Brotherhood removes a subordinate lodge officer from his position; such a case is appealed first to the Board of Directors, and then to the Board of Appeals. In all the cases that go to the Board of Appeals, however, there is no question as to the procedure followed or as to the right of the committee or other authority to take the action it did; the sole issue relates to the merits of the case, to the justice of the action taken.

In its decisions the Board of Appeals tends to uphold the decisions of the various general committees, doubtless reasoning that they are in the best position to know what is obtainable, in view of the agreement and practices on the property. Yet there are a number of cases in which the action of the general committee is reversed, where members of the board feel that considerations of equity so require. In some periods, and in the case of some board members, political considerations evidently have also played a part. Men may be elected to this board, as to any other office, as administration supporters or as anti-administration candidates, and in either case, depending on their personalities and the issues presented to them, their judgment may be influenced by political considerations. The charges filed by Whitney in 1941 against the four of the seven members of the Board of Appeals who reversed his decisions have already been referred to; with the aid of a friendly majority on the Executive Board, Whitney was able to have the four removed from office. In still other types of cases members of the board, being human, may be influenced by considerations other than the simple facts of the case. Thus the activity of a rival union may play a part, in that board members may not wish to antagonize a group of men who might show their displeasure at an adverse decision by leaving the Brotherhood for another union.

Like other Brotherhood agencies with judicial functions, the Board follows due process, asking all interested parties for their views, collecting and reviewing all the documentary material, and affording all parties an opportunity to present their views in person. In disputes between two groups within the union, the statements of each are made available for the other to answer before a decision is reached. Where new evidence becomes available, the case may be reopened for review.

Because railroad rules and practices vary somewhat in the different sections of the country, a system of geographic representation is followed for membership on the Board of Appeals. The board of seven is composed of two members each from the Eastern, the Western, and the Southern territories, and one member from Canada. The Board meets semi-annually and stays in session until its docket of cases has been completed, its members being paid on a per diem basis. This opened the way, as with the Executive Board, for exertion of influence by the president, who might give the board members appointments as organizers for the interim periods. To remove any temptation for board members to curry favor with the president for the sake of such appointments, the constitution was amended in 1954 to provide that members of the Board of Appeals, while serving on it, could not represent the Grand Lodge in any other capacity. The provision has much less impact on the Board of Appeals than on the Executive Board, since the former body tends to be in session for nine to ten months yearly, whereas the latter agency has not heard a case in the past decade.

Until 1950 reports of the Board of Appeals merely showed whether an appeal had been sustained or denied, without disclosing how each member had voted. A very stubborn case had arisen, however, involving the rights of the employees of two railroads in a jointly owned terminal in Kansas City, in which the decision of the Board of Appeals could not be implemented. Unable to get the two general committees to agree on the manner of putting the decision into effect, a Grand Lodge officer recommended, on the basis of new evidence, that the decision be changed, and the president of the Brotherhood followed this recommendation. As an aftermath of this dispute, the question arose as to which way particular members of the Board of Appeals had voted, but this they would not disclose. The 1950 convention, as a result, changed the constitution to require that the way each member voted be shown in each decision. This requirement, needless to say, raises the possibility of reprisal at the following convention against a member whose votes in key cases prove unpopular. While judges generally sign their decisions, they are usually given long tenure of office to safeguard their thinking against the influence of political considerations.

7

Staff Officials

Besides the elected Grand Lodge officers, the Brotherhood has a large number of staff officials, all of them appointed by or in the name of the president, who perform a variety of tasks and who exercise varying degrees of authority. The Field Service Department coordinates the work of vice presidents, deputy presidents, and organizers, the Promotion Department directs the activities of field supervisors, and the Department of Legal Counsel (formerly called the Legal Aid Department) provides legal services to members injured in the service of carriers. Each of these departments involves the employment of a number of Brotherhood members, whose appointments and assignments could have an impact upon the political life of the union. Other officials, such as the head of the Legislative Department, serve as specialists who advise the president with regard to particular types of problems with which he must deal or who handle correspondence or make routine decisions relating to those problems in his name.

Still other officials carry on the varied activities of the union in such fields as research, education, publications, and public relations. The general secretary and treasurer's office requires the work of accountants and auditors, in addition to a large number of clerical employees; with relatively few exceptions, however, these do not come from the ranks of Brotherhood members. The fact that the Brotherhood conducts an insurance business, in addition to the more usual activities of a labor organization, adds to the number of such posts at its national headquarters. A few staff officials are stationed at other points, such as Washington, for the more efficient conduct of certain types of Brotherhood activities.

Apart from the elected officers, the key official at the Grand Lodge offices is the administrative secretary to the president, who helps the president coordinate the work of the various departments. Whitney delegated no such authority; instead he met with his key department heads daily and made assignments directly to each, using a chief clerk for routine matters. While lesser jobs are filled through the seniority system, department heads are selected by the president, either from among Grand Lodge staff members or from the ranks of the Brotherhood. Sometimes elected officers, such as vice presidents or alternate vice presidents, may be appointed to head key departments at Grand Lodge headquarters.

For the permanent positions available at the Grand Lodge headquarters preference is given in the following order: to members of the Brotherhood, to members of its Ladies' Auxiliary, to members of the families of Brotherhood members, and, finally, to others. Complete outsiders are hired when specialized skills are needed or when no applications are available from the preferred categories. The president of the Brotherhood makes the decision in such cases, on the recommendation of the head of the Personnel Department. Resentment is sometimes shown when outsiders are picked for posts, such as editor of the publication, that members might conceivably have filled.[1]

Male employees, except where such specialized skills are needed, come from the ranks of the Brotherhood, starting typically as mail clerks and waiting for vacancies to occur among the better jobs. Grand Lodge employment has the advantages of safety, indoor work, and regularity of employment as compared with work on a railroad, and the basic clerical rate of $503.00 monthly is a little better than a yardman low on the seniority list may expect to earn. Members who have office skills are likely to prefer Grand Lodge employment, as are those who have suffered physical disabilities. As they move up the promotional ladder to the better jobs, which pay annual salaries up to $12,000.00, they are likely to continue to earn somewhat more than they would have received on the railroad. The non-member who becomes a Grand Lodge employee may join the Brotherhood after a period of two years.

Except where specialized training is needed, as for legal or medical positions, the better jobs on the staff are filled by promotion from the lower ranks, with vacancies posted and the senior applicant being given the job unless he lacks the ability to do the work or a junior applicant has outstanding qualifications. This policy, which reflects the importance of seniority among the members of the Brotherhood in their relations with the carriers, may be the cause of some inefficiency in the union's own work, however, since staff positions at the Grand Lodge offices require a far greater variety of skills, sometimes of an administrative or professional nature, than do assignments as trainmen or conductors. Such heavy reliance on the seniority system among its own employees creates a cleavage between the younger employees, who feel held back by it, and the senior employees, who enjoy the benefits. Employees who are dissatisfied with their treatment may utilize grievance machinery negotiated with the Grand Lodge by a committee representing the employees who are Brotherhood members. Though no arbitration provision is available, employees who belong to the Brotherhood may appeal an adverse decision of the president to the Board of Directors, and by inference, even to the convention.

A Grand Lodge employee who comes from the ranks of the Brotherhood may continue to be active in his lodge, provided he is able to attend lodge meetings. He remains eligible to hold any office, though the men would be unlikely to elect him local chairman, since he would be out of touch with conditions on the property. He could be elected delegate to the convention, provided he met the qualifications of insurance membership and attendance at the required number of meetings, and this has happened several times in recent years. He could also be elected, in exceptional cases, to Grand Lodge office, as was the case with two officers elected at the 1960 convention. In most cases, however, career employment with the Grand Lodge is not the way to an elected office. Except for the holders of the top staff positions,

Grand Lodge employees tend to avoid political work, since they want to keep their employment, and to have good relations with the officers, regardless of the outcome of elections.

Deputy Presidents and Organizers

The assignment of deputy presidents and organizers is a function of the Field Service Department at Grand Lodge headquarters. Requests for aid come to the president from general chairmen who want Grand Lodge help in their grievance handling or negotiating problems or in the building up of membership on the property. The work of handling problems with management is assigned to a vice president or to a deputy president, who enjoys the authority of a vice president and is paid at the same rate, while the task of contacting members or prospective members is given to organizers. Deputy presidents may be assigned at first for periods of perhaps 30, 45, or 90 days, with their assignments gradually lengthened until finally they may go on full-time service. The period of service of an organizer, by way of contrast, is usually 10 days or less, though some serve for longer periods and occasionally one is employed in that capacity throughout the year. As of November 1, 1959, deputy presidents were being paid at the daily rate of $42.74, which amounted to about $15,600.00 for one on service throughout the entire year, while organizers were being paid at the rate of $28.40 a day.

Deputy presidents are chosen for their experience and ability in collective bargaining. Usually they are general chairmen or former general chairmen, though in some cases they may be outstanding local chairmen. A general chairman of a large road is not likely to be appointed a deputy president, since he may be unable to spare the time that this assignment requires. Because of the importance of the position, and also the high pay that goes with it, an appointment as deputy president is unlikely to be made without regard to political considerations, along with the required experience and ability; a political opponent of the president cannot expect an appointment as deputy president, nor is a former supporter who breaks with the president likely to continue long in such an important and highly paid post.

When a request for Grand Lodge assistance in negotiations

with management is made by a general chairman, the head of the Field Service Department may assign the vice president of that area, another vice president, or a deputy president, the choice depending upon the availability of the officers and the nature of the assignment. If the problem arises on a specialized type of carrier, such as a steel carrying railroad company, an officer familiar with the operations of such roads would be assigned. If the issue is a highly controversial one within the Brotherhood, such as a dispute between two general committees over the allocation of work, or a wildcat strike in which someone may have to be disciplined, the tendency is to assign a deputy president rather than an elected officer, who may be too much concerned with his chances for re-election. The vice president of the area must continue to work with the local officers and committees, moreover, while the deputy president, who may be assigned anywhere in the country, may be moved elsewhere if a particular action of his proves unpopular with local groups.

Yet the deputy president cannot act in an arbitrary fashion, or an appeal will be taken to the Board of Appeals and his action reversed. A deputy president to whom this happens a number of times loses his effectiveness, and becomes a liability rather than an asset to the president. The deputy president, moreover, may be ambitious for a vice presidential post, and hope that his actions in the field will build up his circle of friends and increase his popularity with the membership. In a collective bargaining situation a deputy president, like a vice president, is authorized to sign an agreement without requiring further approval; in other cases, however, his authority is limited to making a recommendation to the president. Management may be happier with a vice president, who may not want much controversy in his territory; a deputy president, on the other hand, may be trying to build a record, through concessions from management, to improve his chances of winning an elected post at the next convention.

Organizers are appointed for shorter periods, often for merely two to five days, to the task of building up membership on the road or countering the activities of a rival union. Trouble may start when dissatisfied men stop paying dues (where no union shop is in effect, though such clauses now exist on most railroads) or contact a rival union, or when an officer who is defeated for re-election goes over to a rival union, seeking to carry his following with him. Authorization cards of a rival union may be circulated, or one of its representatives may appear on the property. As soon as it is evident to the officers of the lodge that trouble is brewing, they will inform the general chairman, who in turn may ask the president of the Brotherhood to assign an organizer to the area. If an election is pending on an important road, with the Brotherhood seeking either to retain or to win representation rights, a large number of organizers may be used. Since union shop and check-off provisions have spread on the railroads, there has been less occasion for the use of organizers, because men who stop paying dues may risk the loss of their jobs, unless they can satisfy the requirements of the union shop by joining another union.

If another union is trying to take representation rights away from the Brotherhood, the most influential organizers are likely to be leading local chairmen of the lodges on the road. If the Brotherhood is trying to win bargaining rights from another union, a combination of Brotherhood officers in the area and dissatisfied officers of the union that has represented the men in the past may be most effective. Sometimes, when the Brotherhood loses bargaining rights, skeletal lodges of the men most loyal to the Brotherhood are kept alive until a representation challenge may again be made; in such cases officers of these lodges are the most logical candidates for appointments as organizers. If it is a case of dissatisfaction among the membership of one or more Brotherhood lodges, on the other hand, the lodge officers who are most loyal to the Brotherhood, and most influential among the men, are likely to prove the most successful organizers. A man who has been elected a number of times to lodge office is a potential organizer, since repeated elections show that he enjoys influence and has a following among the men. To be successful, an organizer must have an acceptable personality, along with patience and discretion; he must be popular among and respected by the men on the road; he must also be willing to work, and must conduct himself so as to deserve the confidence of the men and reflect credit upon the organization.

The appointment as organizer carries a certain amount of recognition and prestige and constitutes a welcome break in the normal work routine of a conductor or brakeman, even though it is the least desirable type of appointment at the disposal of the Grand Lodge. The local officers most likely to be appointed organizers, it should be noted, are also among those most likely to be elected delegates to the convention. Such appointments, limited as they are in length, pay, and prestige, may, nevertheless, be welcome enough to the recipients to make them more likely to vote to retain the administration that appointed them. From this point of view the appointments constitute political assets of no little importance to any administration.

Suggestions of men to be appointed organizers come to the Grand Lodge from general chairmen, field supervisors, vice presidents, and deputy presidents. Field supervisors become involved because their work is to bring in new members, as well as to sell insurance both to new and to old members. To the extent that the organizer is approaching potential new members, he may stress the insurance program along with the protective work of the Brotherhood. The general chairman is the one most likely to recommend the appointment of particular men at particular times, since he is responsible for the protection of Brotherhood interests on the road and since his budget usually provides half the cost. He may discuss the matter with the field supervisor in the area, however, and agree with the supervisor upon names before submitting them to the Grand Lodge.

If the president disapproves of suggested organizers, either he or the general chairman may suggest other names until agreement is reached. It would be unlikely for a president to name an organizer who was not acceptable to the general chairman, since a lack of cooperation between the two would hold little promise of success, and since the general chairman would not want to use his funds to pay part of the salary of an organizer of whose appointment he disapproved. In practice the head of the Field Service Department acts for and in the name of the president in the appointment of organizers. The department keeps a file of names of members who have been used or suggested for use as organizers. Once their names have been cleared with the president, the head of the department is free to appoint them as needed, unless their services prove unacceptable or unless the president for any reasons withdraws his approval.

There is no limit, other than the president's discretion and the size of the treasury, to the number of deputy presidents and organizers who may be appointed. As has already been pointed out, the number of deputy presidents appointed in the course of a year may vary from a dozen or less to a hundred or more, depending on organizational needs. In 1946, when the Trainmen engaged in a nationwide strike under peculiarly difficult conditions, involving a controversy with the president of the United States, a total of 409 deputy presidents were appointed. At other times, when there happen to be few bargaining problems with the carriers, the Brotherhood's needs may be met by half a dozen or so deputy presidents. The number of organizers appointed in the course of a year has fluctuated in recent years from just under 1,000 to well over 2,000, most of these appointments being for just a few days each.

Appointments as deputy presidents and as organizers may have an influence on the internal political life of the union, since the sheer bulk of organizers' commissions issued makes it likely that a number of the approximately 1,100 delegates to a convention have received such appointments. One can only speculate as to whether, and to what extent, their voting behavior may have been influenced by the bits of patronage they may have enjoyed. There has also been some suspicion that deputy presidents and organizers, as well as field supervisors, might be used for political purposes at conventions, as witness the motion offered on the second day of the 1960 convention that any such officers receiving wages from the Grand Lodge while attending the convention be sent home.[2]

Field Supervisors and Legal Counsel

Two additional departments of the Brotherhood, the Promotion Department and the Department of Legal Counsel, were created to service the membership outside the collective bargaining and grievance sphere of operations. The Promotion Department, which consists of an insurance counselor and a manager with his aides at Grand Lodge headquarters, 52 field supervisors, and one or more insurance representatives in each subordinate lodge, has the dual function of building up membership and selling insurance. From its inception as a benevolent organization the Brotherhood has met the insurance needs of men in a hazardous occupation at rates equivalent to or lower than those charged by commercial companies, with policies tailored to railroad workers' needs, and with a more sympathetic policy with regard to the payment of claims.

The other department, dealing with legal aid, was organized to serve the interests of members who suffered accidents in the course of their work, and who needed competent and reputable legal representation at reasonable fees. Prior to this time some members had felt obliged to sign away their rights for fear of offending their employers, whereas others had fallen victim to unscrupulous lawyers. The Brotherhood's Department of Legal Counsel consists of a manager at the Cleveland Grand Lodge offices and 21 lawyers or law firms scattered throughout the country, who are available to represent members of the union. Subordinate lodge officers may suggest to an injured member of the Brotherhood that he be represented in his claim for damages by the union's legal counsel in the area. Some of the lawyers have on their staffs investigators, who typically are Trainmen members, for use in cases where practical railroad experience would be valuable.

The plan of using field supervisors to sell Brotherhood insurance policies to the membership got its start in 1931, when the union changed its insurance system from an assessment to a reserve basis. Until this time every member was required to belong to the Insurance Department, the insurance aspect of membership being handled by the local lodge officers without commission or other additional compensation. When insurance was made optional, however, a sales organization was needed to sell the policies. At first many of the field supervisors were professional insurance men, though in the last twenty years or so all of the appointees have come from the ranks of the Brotherhood.

Appointments as field supervisor are made by the Individual Reserve Board, which consists of the president, the assistant to the president, and the general secretary and treasurer. In practice this usually means that the president controls the appointment, though recommendations may be made to him by the manager of the Promotion Department or by others. Members who have served as insurance representatives in their lodges may file applications for the post of field supervisor, and others may be suggested by general chairmen, vice presidents, or state legislative representatives. Where the positions promise to be lucrative ones, political considerations may also be involved, since a president, in making his choice, is likely to know which candidates have been his supporters in the past or are likely to be useful to him in the future. To be successful a field supervisor must have a pleasing personality, be able to get along with people, and have an aptitude for selling.

For such a person an appointment as field supervisor in a thickly populated and strongly organized area can be both satisfying and remunerative. The work is much to be preferred— for someone who enjoys working with people—to a job as brakeman or conductor, and the earnings are much higher in a desirable territory. A field supervisor, who receives no salary, is paid a small sum for each new member in his territory, and receives a percentage of the premiums paid over a ten-year period on all insurance policies that he writes. For the period of 1950 through June, 1954, the field supervisors had average annual gross earnings of $17,657.00, and net earnings, after the payment of expenses, of $8,520.00.[3] The most successful field supervisors now have gross commission earnings of $20,000.00 or even more annually, out of which their expenses for travel, hiring assistants, etc., must be paid. Their income depends, not only on their sales ability and their willingness to work hard, but also on the territories assigned them. The one who works in a large, sparsely settled territory must spend more time and money in travel than the one in a compact, thickly settled, area. On the average each field supervisor has about twenty lodges with approximately three thousand members in his territory. His business may require the appointment of one or two assistant field supervisors, who work under his direction and maintain close contact with the insurance representatives in these lodges.

Almost every lodge, excepting only some very small ones, has one or more insurance representatives, appointed by the head of the Promotion Department. The most likely person is the treasurer, who must handle payments and receipts anyway, and who usually certifies claims that are submitted when men are sick or injured. In other cases lodge presidents, secretaries, local chairmen, or former officers serve as insurance representatives. They receive small payments for new members, plus commissions on the first year premiums on the policies they help to sell. Where there are two or more seniority districts in a lodge, each is likely to have its own insurance representative, who writes policies for the men with whom he works. A typical insurance representative may receive $25.00 to $35.00 monthly for this work, with the most successful ones earning up to perhaps $200.00.

A field supervisor enjoys no security either in his appointment or in his assigned territory, since his contract may be terminated on thirty days' notice and since his territory may be reduced or otherwise changed at any time. The only field supervisor who can be independent of the president, therefore, is one who is within a decade of retirement, and who has made enough sales in recent years to be assured of a satisfactory income until he is eligible for his pension under the railroad retirement system. A field supervisor must also consider the sentiment of the key officers and membership in his area, however. He may keep his appointment by following the instructions of the Grand Lodge, though if the result is unpopularity in his area his chances of a good selling record, and therefore of a satisfactory income, will be reduced materially.

Field supervisors are apt to know the sentiments of the membership better than any other group of officers, since they get into the homes as well as the lodge meeting halls and build friendly relationships with the men as a result of handling some of their personal problems. Relations of the men with general chairmen and the state legislative representatives are likely to be more impersonal, limited to the problems within their particular areas of competence.

It is widely believed within the union that field supervisors are used from time to time for political purposes, to sound out membership opinion on a touchy political issue or to influence members to vote for or against particular candidates. This is denied by other Brotherhood officials, who assert that those field supervisors who participate in politics do so on their own volition, without receiving Grand Lodge instructions to follow. What is beyond question is that political activity by field supervisors, where it occurs, is widely resented.

Field supervisors who are not delegates, but who, nevertheless, attend conventions, do so at their own expense, looking upon the cost of attending and of entertaining delegates from their area as a type of good will expenditure likely to pay off in good relations and, therefore, higher insurance commissions in the future. In one case, however, they received payment from the Grand Lodge for attendance; General Secretary and Treasurer Weil advised the delegates to the 1960 convention that each field supervisor had received the sum of $1,250.00 after the 1954 convention.[4] The political influence of field supervisors, understandably enough, has become a controversial issue within the Brotherhood. At several conventions there has been some sentiment for abolishing the positions, and at others proposals have been made, as was the case in 1960, that field supervisors receiving pay from the Grand Lodge while in attendance be sent home. It should be remembered, however, that field supervisors were receiving income from commissions on insurance policies previously sold.

The lawyers who are associated with the Department of Legal Counsel are in a more independent position than the field supervisors, in that their practice is not restricted to Brotherhood members and the loss of the Brotherhood connection does not confront them with the unpleasant alternative open to the field supervisor. Yet the Brotherhood affiliation is a lucrative one, because of the large sums recovered in accident cases. In the years 1946 through 1949, a total of 2,431 settlements were negotiated and $26,719,000.00 collected through attorneys connected with the department, while members received $14,242,000.00 additional through the direct settlement of 8,003 cases.[5] Since then, from 500 to 700 cases have been closed yearly by lawyers associated with the department. The lawyer gets one-fourth of the sums collected through his efforts, making for a very substantial income.

Some of the money spent for the entertainment of delegates at state meetings or international union conventions originates with the lawyers, who may welcome opportunities to mingle socially with prospective clients. Sometimes lawyers may provide the liquid refreshments for "hospitality" rooms at state gatherings or they may entertain convention delegates from their districts at dinners, all in the effort to build friendly relations and thereby increase the likelihood of future business. In such activities, however, they must watch the rules established by the Bar Association. It is believed by some members of the union that a portion of the funds spent by the administration for political purposes originates with the lawyers, and that some of these may be willing to help finance an opposition candidate as well, to be assured of friendly relations with the president however the election turns out. It is not possible to verify, much less document, reports of this sort.

In addition to the customary channels of influence and communication available to the national head of any union, the president of the Brotherhood may, therefore, derive political advantage, in ways not easily checked, from two additional sets of appointees—the field supervisors and the legal counsel. It would be ironic if these two groups of officers, appointed to provide unusual types of service to members of the Brotherhood outside the union payroll, should have evolved into agencies through which political influence might be exerted over the membership.

8

The Convention

The convention, which normally meets every fourth year, is the supreme political power in the union, determining policy as well as electing the national officers; when it is in session, it is the Grand Lodge, which under Section 6 of the constitution "has exclusive jurisdiction over all subjects pertaining to the Brotherhood, and its enactments and decisions upon all questions are the supreme law of the Brotherhood." Until 1960 the constitution provided that "The Grand Lodge shall meet quadrennially"; because of the controversy that arose over whether this language was mandatory, the wording was changed that year to read that "The Grand Lodge must meet in 1964 and quadrennially thereafter." Special conventions may be called by the president or ordered by referendum vote. A special convention may act only on those subjects for which it has been called, unless it resolves itself into a regular convention.

Such a situation occurred in 1960, when a special convention was called by Kennedy for two purposes—to make the constitution conform to the new federal law, and to elect Grand Lodge officers. Once the convention met it quickly decided, under pressure from the insurgent group, to remove the word "Special" from the convention call. This vote, which was taken without a roll call, was a poor index to the sentiment of the delegates on the factional alignment, however, since a delegate was easily persuaded to remain in Cleveland for the full six-week period usually devoted to a regular convention rather than stay merely for the limited business of a special convention.

The Delegates

Convention delegates, who are elected for four-year periods, represent their lodges at any special convention that may be called during that time. To be eligible to serve as convention delegate, a member must have been an insurance member during the previous year, must hold seniority in some class of service represented by the Brotherhood, and must have attended at least three meetings a year for the preceding three years and six meetings in the year the election was held. He must also have served for at least three years in the aggregate in some elective office or on some elective committee. He cannot hold membership in any other railroad or bus labor organization, or be employed by the carrier as an assistant yardmaster or in a higher rating. While these rather stringent eligibility rules limit sharply the number of members eligible to serve, they assure the presence at a convention of active and informed delegates.

To be elected delegate is considered both an honor and a reward—an honor in that one can help to decide the future policies of the Brotherhood, and a reward for years of work, most of it unpaid, in the interests of the lodge. The compensation paid delegates and the fairly short working hours, allowing opportunity for recreation, are considered partly as a return to the most valuable officer of the lodge for service rendered over a period of years. A Grand Lodge officer is not eligibile to represent his lodge as a delegate; he is entitled to a voice, but not a vote, at the convention. Delegates are not bound by any instructions given them by their lodges.

Of the 1,122 delegates at the 1960 convention 998 held lodge office—369 as local chairman, 246 as legislative representative, 163 as secretary and treasurer, 75 as president, 73 as treasurer, and

72 as secretary. The small number who held the office of president shows the relative unimportance of that position within the Brotherhood. There is a tendency, where a lodge is composed of a single seniority district, for the local chairman, as the most important officer of the lodge, to be elected delegate. Where a number of seniority districts are included, however, the delegate is more likely to be an officer such as the secretary and treasurer (if those offices are combined) or the legislative representative, who deals with the entire membership.

The 1,122 delegates in 1960 included 410 passenger, yard, or freight conductors, 248 passenger, yard, or freight brakemen, 176 yard brakemen, 171 yard conductors, 32 bus operators, 25 general chairmen, 18 baggagemen, 8 switchtenders, 7 field supervisors, 6 yardmasters, 6 dining car stewards or conductors, 4 legal aid investigators, 4 retarder operators, 2 legislative representatives, 2 yard clerks, 1 dispatcher, 1 towerman, and 1 motorman. Until 1954, when the requirement that delegates must hold seniority in a class of service represented by the Brotherhood was added to the constitution, a group of retired men came as delegates, along with occasional members then in such miscellaneous occupations as real estate broker, postmaster, owner of a bottling plant, state inspector, motion picture operator, church official, floor manager of a department store, electrical engineer, and private detective.[1]

Each subordinate lodge, regardless of size, is entitled to one delegate with one vote at conventions—a policy which makes it possible for a minority of the membership, grouped in small lodges, to outvote the majority. There has been some dissatisfaction with this method of allocating votes, as witness the resolution introduced at the 1960 convention to amend the constitution to assign one vote to a lodge with fewer than one hundred members, and one vote for each one hundred members or balance thereof to larger locals.[2]

The tradition of the Trainmen is to have long conventions, lasting six or seven weeks. While conventions of this length allow the delegates ample time to debate policy issues, revise the constitution, and become acquainted with candidates for office, the resulting cost, in the neighborhood of $2,500,000.00, is far out of proportion to the benefits achieved, particularly for a union with fewer than 200,000 members. The 1960 convention, the most expensive in the union's history, cost well over $3,000,000.00. In all likelihood the convention period could be shortened materially, and the cost of conventions substantially reduced, without any great danger to the quality of the work accomplished. Several attempts have been made, without success, to reduce the length of conventions. Delegates have voted to read every section of the constitution, however, though in one case the lodges voted, prior to the convention, that only sections for which changes were recommended by the resolutions committee be read.

Until after 1913 no convention of the Brotherhood had lasted longer than 17 days. Then the length began to increase—to 26 days in 1916, 30 in 1922, 37 in 1931, 48 in 1939, and 52, the all-time record, in 1946. The three conventions since then have lasted between 40 and 46 days each. This steady increase in convention length seems to have been due, not to any corresponding increase in the volume of business, but rather to the fact that the delegates, enjoying the change from their usual work routines, were in no hurry to leave. Nor is the president, who stands for re-election near the end of the convention, likely to risk antagonizing delegates by speeding up the convention tempo.

The constitution provides that delegates receive pay for their services at a rate not to exceed $17.00 per day for a day of six hours or less, with pay at time and a half for night sessions and overtime, and with a per diem allowance as determined by the convention. At the 1960 convention daily pay of $17.00 and a $35.00 per diem allowance were fixed; the per diem was $25.00 at the 1954 convention and $20.00 in 1950, in addition to a daily salary of $15.00. A delegate who is absent at roll call or when the yeas and nays are called on any subject receives no pay for that day, unless he is sick or has been excused by the convention. Members of convention committees receive additional payments. Convention expenses are charged against the Brotherhood's various funds, including the protective fund, the general fund, and the Insurance Department, in proportion to the time spent on the corresponding subjects. To the outside observer the short working day, the provision of time and a half for overtime, the additional pay for committee duty, and the high per diem allowance all appear to increase the cost of conventions without any corresponding benefit to the membership of the union.

Convention Committees

Conventions of the Trainmen rely on committees for the performance of a large part of their work. For the 1960 convention, for example, nineteen committees were appointed, dealing respectively with constitution and general rules, reports of Grand Lodge officers, legislation—United States, legislation—Canada, official publication—*Trainman News,* salaries, ritual and secret work, organization, convention, reception, sickness, appeals, resolutions—United States, resolutions—Canada, miles and hours, bus problems, dining car stewards—United States, dining car stewards—Canada, and relations with the Firemen. Most committees consisted of 5 members each, a total of 108 members serving on these committees. Except for the committees on constitution and on reports of Grand Lodge officers, which are appointed by the Board of Directors, a majority of all committees is appointed by the president, and the remainder by the assistant to the president. The president also designates the chairman of each of these committees, with the committee selecting its own secretary. The committees on constitution, reports of Grand Lodge officers, and resolutions begin their meetings well in advance of the convention. The credentials committee, by constitutional provision, consists of the assistant to the president, the senior vice president, and the general secretary and treasurer.

In addition to the 108 members of the committees dealing with substantive matters at the 1960 convention, 33 served on the committee manning the voting machines, and large numbers were appointed as guards, to see that only delegates were allowed on the floor of the convention. Though the hall had only eight entrances, a total of 203 guards were appointed, making a total of 344 delegates serving as committee members or guards.[3] The guards alternated their periods on duty, from 24 to 31 serving each week. At the 1954 convention, by way of contrast, only 40 delegates had been assigned as guards.

The number of guards, and also the compensation paid them, became a controversial issue at the 1960 convention, since the insurgent group feared that such appointments constituted a form of patronage, controlled by the administration, that might influence doubtful votes. By vote on the second day of the convention, five dollars per day was fixed as the additional compensation paid to delegates serving on committees. On the eighteenth day, when the insurgent group feared that the large number of guards might be a factor in swinging the convention against them, a motion was made and carried that guards be paid only for the days that they were on duty; otherwise, the antiadministration group feared, all the guards might receive the additional five dollars daily for the entire period of the convention.

A motion was then offered that all committee members be paid on the same basis, but Kennedy refused to accept the motion, on the ground that all committees were working daily. Another motion was made that committee chairmen report the number of days that their committees were in session, and that the committee members be paid for that number of days; this motion was defeated,[4] with the result that committee members received the additional daily compensation for the entire period of the convention. The 1954 convention, by way of contrast, had voted that the additional allowances of four dollars daily to committee members be paid only up to and including the day the committees finished their work.[5]

Convention Actions

Many union conventions, rather than serving as deliberative assemblies to formulate policies, appear to be demonstrations of solidarity, and agencies to ratify programs determined in advance. The top officers, referred to with affection and gratitude, and re-elected unanimously, are in complete control; differences of opinion, where they occur, are compromised in committees or by key personnel behind the scenes, seldom erupting on the convention floor. Trainmen conventions are not of this type, although the presence of 1,100 or more delegates makes for a body of somewhat unwieldy size. There is no question, at a convention of the Brotherhood, that policy differences are fought out in floor debate and resolved by vote, and that the delegates, by majority vote, decide, within broad limits, the policies that the organization is to follow. The leaders of the union, depending upon a favorable convention vote for re-election and usually facing opposition candidates, cater to the delegates rather than the other way around. The length of the convention, allowing time for the leisurely debate of all important issues, plays an important part in this, though traditions of the Brotherhood also exert an influence.

Nowhere is the difference between Brotherhood conventions and those of many other unions more apparent than in the revision of the constitution, the basic document that defines the powers of officers in relationship to union policy and the rights of members. Because of the press of time, the important task of considering revision of the constitution is referred to a committee in the Brotherhood, as it is in other unions; but whereas many union conventions have only a limited time for debate and vote on constitutional changes, often merely adopting reports proposed by the committee, the Brotherhood goes through its constitution, section by section and line by line, at every convention. It does this in Committee of the Whole, for which it elects its own chairman—sometimes, as in 1960, rejecting the candidate proposed by the administration in order to elect an insurgent candidate.

This procedure is followed despite the fact that a committee on the constitution meets about ninety days prior to the convention to consider changes that have been suggested by subordinate lodges or by Grand Lodge officers. Its report on recommended changes goes to subordinate lodges forty-five days before the convention opens, so that delegates have ample time to become familiar with the issues involved before they assemble for the convention. Further changes may be suggested early in the convention or when the convention is considering the report. A majority vote—two-thirds until 1950—is sufficient to amend the constitution. This detailed examination of the constitution by the entire body of delegates consumes a great deal of time, duplicating the work of the committee on the constitution and adding materially to the expense of a convention, though it also serves as a constant reminder that the delegates, by majority vote, control the destinies of the organization.

Convention resolutions, which may be introduced by lodge action or on the initiative of delegates, express the union's attitude on a wide variety of subjects. Some of the resolutions relate to collective bargaining issues, stating objectives that may require national wage or rules movements for their attainment or that may be won individually on each road; on some of the latter issues, such as mileage limitation, the convention has the choice of stating a national standard or of allowing each general committee to define its own objective in the light of its particular situation. Collective bargaining resolutions may relate to levels of pay, arbitrary allowances for additional duties, hours of work, seniority lists, pay differentials, work guarantees, protection of furloughed men, or any other subjects that may be included in negotiations with the carriers. Other resolutions may constitute statements of legislative policy, on such issues as safety, railroad retirement, hours of work, or regulation of the carriers by the Interstate Commerce Commission or by state agencies. Still other convention pronouncements may set internal union policy with regard to insurance programs, the union paper, educational activities, or a retirement plan for union officers; or they may state the union's position on broad issues confronting the nation, ranging from efforts to achieve full employment to foreign policy.

The convention is also the highest judicial body of the union, its decisions settling issues on the interpretation of the constitution or the powers of officers or committees within the union structure. Such issues, if they relate to decisions by the president, are appealed first to the Board of Directors and then to the convention; or, if they deal with the power of a general committee, for example, to take a particular action, they go first to the president, then to the Board of Directors, and finally to the convention. Appeals handled by the Board of Directors may always be appealed to the convention.

Appeals that go from the president to the Board of Appeals, involving the merits of actions taken by a general committee on grievances or collective bargaining issues, are decided finally by the Board of Appeals, with no right of appeal to the convention; by a two-thirds vote, however, the convention may assume jurisdiction over the issue. A Grand Lodge officer who has been removed by the Executive Board may appeal its decision directly to the convention. Appeals are considered by the convention's Committee on Appeals, which hears delegates and other interested parties before reporting its recommendations to the convention floor, where the final decision is made.

Cases decided on appeal by recent conventions have involved such issues as: the negotiation by general committees of agreements on working conditions, compulsory retirement, or mileage limitations, or their actions in removing a general chairman or closing out time claims; the election of delegates to a convention; the question as to whether members of a state legislative board properly belonged there; actions of the president of the Brotherhood in removing subordinate lodge officers, resubmitting a case to the Board of Appeals, changing the salaries of Grand Lodge employees, establishing an arbitration board, and using the 1954 delegates for the 1960 convention; and the removal of Grand Lodge officers by the Executive Board. In other types of cases the convention has refused to review decisions by the Board of Appeals on the merits of work disputes, on the ground that that board's decisions finally settled such cases under the union's constitution; it has referred to the Board of Appeals for further consideration a conflict between two lodges over the division of work; and it has dismissed appeals from actions of the president in cases involving the closing out of claims by a general committee, on the ground that the proper avenue of appeal in such cases was to the Board of Appeals.

Political Activities and the Election of Officers

Brotherhood conventions have been the scene of spirited political activities, as preceding chapters have shown. Eleven of the last fifteen conventions, covering the years from 1909 to 1960, inclusive, have seen contests for the presidency, as for many of the lesser offices. Candidates have held meetings of their supporters, as Smith did during the years that he contested the presidency, first against Whitney and then against Kennedy. There was no organized factional activity prior to or subsequent to conventions, however, until the Committee of the Hundred formed as an anti-Kennedy group in 1959, to be replaced by the 460 Club following the 1960 convention.

The 1960 convention witnessed perhaps the most open factional activity in the history of the Brotherhood. As delegates arrived in Cleveland on January 3, they were greeted in each hotel with large signs, inviting them to attend a preconvention meeting that evening. The meeting was sponsored by a group of anti-administration delegates from Pennsylvania calling themselves the Committee for a Consitutional Convention. A leaflet distributed to arriving delegates asserted:

We are convinced our organization is in the hands of "tired old men" whose only desire is to perpetuate themselves in office by hook or crook.

The "tired old men" of the Grand Lodge will use all sorts of tricks and legal hair-splitting to take the convention away from us unless we are prepared to protect ourselves. . . .

If we don't want to be rushed out of Cleveland, if we don't believe in rigged conventions, if we believe a convention belongs to the delegates, then a few hours of our time on January 3rd may be very profitable to us during the convention.

The preconvention meeting sponsored by the Committee for a Constitutional Convention attracted approximately 600 of the 1,100 delegates. While the size of the turn-out undoubtedly encouraged the insurgent group, it was clear that the audience included a number of administration supporters who had come to hear what the opposition had to say, plus many uncommitted delegates who wanted to hear the arguments of both sides before giving their support to either. If the meeting showed that the insurgents enjoyed widespread delegate support, however, it also demonstrated that their support among the top leadership of the union was very limited. The meeting was devoted to an attack upon Kennedy's leadership of the union during the preceding years. Subsequent meetings of the Committee were announced at the convention sessions.

Factional literature, some of it anonymous and some of it signed, has been distributed at conventions throughout the Brotherhood's history. A few samples will show the outspoken quality of these documents. An anonymous anti-Lee leaflet, for which many believed Whitney to be partly responsible, was distributed at the 1907 convention, while Morrissey was still president. Headed "Czar Lee Must Go!," the leaflet urged delegates: "Break the ring that has existed since 1895! No more four-flushing for ours!" [6]

Political literature distributed during the Whitney era showed the same outspoken quality, despite Whitney's well-known tendency to file charges against those who crossed him. At the 1946 convention, for example, a bluntly worded six-page mimeographed statement was distributed in the interests of Smith's candidacy, though it bore no signature, being signed only "The Rebels" and "The S.I.G. Club" (standing for "Silence Is Golden"). Yet it would probably not have been too difficult to track down the authors or distributors of the statement, and in many unions such efforts would undoubtedly have been made, and those responsible, if their connection were established, placed under charges. It is significant that no such effort was made.

The flavor of this 1946 document is shown by the following extracts:

Our Organization has ceased to exist as a Labor or Fraternal Organization or for the interests of the members, but instead has been transformed into a commercial insurance racket and the building up of a Dictatorship controlled by a dominating bureaucratic leader who enjoys being called the President. . . .

Before his term of office expired he had eliminated all Officers and members who opposed his aspiration to Dictatorship and has carried on with those who forgot your interests for their own financial gain. . . .

He has compared himself rightfully with Hitler; he has termed himself the Czar; he has ruled by favor and is mixed up with the Communists; he has built up a Gestapo in the Field Supervisors and His Deputies, and as Past President Bill Lee said he would, Rule or Ruin.

By domination of Executive power and drafts on our Brotherhood treasury, he has now piled up a mass confusion beyond human comprehension, impossible of Democratic control, extravagant, wasteful, inefficient, and in its nature the instrumentality of favoritism, tyranny, oppression and corruption, and is the destroyer of self-reliance, self-respect and executive capacity of the membership and Local Lodges without which no organization can remain free or progress.

The political literature distributed at the 1960 convention was equally blunt. In the foreword to his pamphlet, *Our Fight for Democracy,* Clyde Titler stated in part:

As you read President Kennedy's sworn testimony you will be amazed by the following

1. His lack of knowledge of Brotherhood affairs.

2. His dictatorial, arrogant, "I am the law!" attitude.

3. His acting as though he *owned* the Brotherhood of Railroad Trainmen.

Extracts from the testimony in the Ohio case, which followed, were headed, "Here's How President Kennedy Twisted the Constitution . . . in the Ohio Hearing." [7]

Another circular, distributed at the convention by Frank Mead, a member of the Brotherhood, was headed "An Open Letter to President Kennedy, B of R T." After charging Kennedy with silence on the featherbedding issue and with placing a large number of unproductive and highly-paid officials on the union payroll, Mead concluded:

> The Brotherhood and its members have treated you fairly and with great generosity—far out of proportion to your abilities.
> How have you treated the Brotherhood and its members? We need capable, physically-fit representation. . . . You are probably tired and in need of rest.
> You have reached the good old age of 67.
> Don't you think it's time to go?
> The members think so. I've heard them say so.

The important thing about these publications, from the point of view of the present discussion, is not whether particular statements are accurate or justified or not, but that a number of members have the courage to put such views on paper, signing their names and lodge numbers, and give their publications wide distribution.

The Grand Lodge officers are elected one at a time by the convention, beginning with the president, and going down the list of other officers roughly in the order of their importance. To be elected, a candidate must receive a majority vote. On the first ballot all those with a small number of votes, such as under fifty, may be eliminated, and on each subsequent ballot the low man is dropped until an election is had. The election is conducted with the aid of voting machines, with the secrecy of the ballot protected, and with each candidate privileged to appoint a watcher. At the 1960 convention each candidate was allowed to speak for two minutes before the vote was taken. A defeated candidate, without loss of prestige, may run for lesser offices until he is elected to one or becomes discouraged. Open meetings in support of candidates are held in the evenings, with all delegates invited.

The most important officers, all of whom are elected at the convention, include the president, the assistant to the president, the general secretary and treasurer, the assistant general secretary and treasurer, the national legislative representative, the Canadian legislative representative, fifteen vice presidents, a Board of Trustees and Insurance of three, and a Board of Appeals of seven.

The vice presidencies are numbered and the incumbents traditionally run for their old offices, moving up to the next higher one as a vacancy occurs. The 1960 convention, besides combining two formerly separate boards into the Board of Trustees and Insurance, provided for eight alternate vice presidents, in addition to alternates for many of the other posts, to be elevated automatically in the event of the death, retirement, or resignation of the incumbent. In addition there is an Executive Board of five, though these positions require little time and allow payment only when duties are performed. While these posts are at the disposal of the convention, the president has a great deal of influence, particularly with respect to the more important positions. His endorsement is sought eagerly by ambitious men who think that their service to him, plus their qualifications and their popularity, entitle them to his support.

If the president decides to support a particular candidate, word is passed to the administration supporters, while disappointed candidates have the choice of running anyway, thereby risking defeat and perhaps incurring the president's displeasure, or withdrawing in the hope of better luck in the future. Sometimes the president, instead of making a choice, will say that either of two or more candidates is acceptable to him, and let their popularity with the delegates determine the issue. Upon occasion, indeed, this happens even where spirited opposition candidates are in the field. Since it takes a majority vote to elect to any office, nothing is lost by permitting the administration vote to be divided among two or more candidates in the early balloting, so long as all the president's supporters rally in the end to the administration candidate who makes the best showing. The leader of an antiadministration bloc may follow a similar practice, and in both cases the decision may be made either by the top leader alone or by the leader in association with a handful of trusted aides.

The importance of presidential approval weakens, however, as one passes from the more important Grand Lodge offices to the lesser ones. Most delegates are not disciplined voters, even though they may sympathize in a general way with the administration or with an opposition group. As the voting proceeds, they respond less and less to wishes of the head of the ticket, voting their own preferences instead. A vice president who has made unpopular settlements may receive few votes from the delegates from his area, even though they may be staunch supporters of the president with whose blessing he runs. The delegates, moreover, may be impressed with the qualities of the candidate whom they defeated for the presidency and elect him to another high Brotherhood office, despite efforts of the president to keep his defeated rival from any Grand Lodge office.

Each presidential candidate is likely to have an informal steering committee at the convention, a group of influential officers who support his candidacy and who recommend strategy to be followed on convention issues. They also seek to build up support, on key convention votes as well as in the elections, for the proposals or nominations that have been decided upon. General chairmen, state legislative representatives, vice presidents, and other influential officers, whether delegates to the convention or not, may help the candidate of their choice in this way.

Delegates respond not only to the personalities, programs, and records of achievement of candidates for high Brotherhood office but also to a series of other pressures and influences. They may be grateful to the president for appointments as organizer in the past, or resentful because they did not receive such appointments. Delegates with greater experience may hope for appointment to more important posts, such as deputy president, or for the president's support, when the time is ripe, for a Grand Lodge elective post. Others may be resentful because they were passed over for such positions in the past. Rank-and-file delegates may be pleased to have been appointed members of a convention committee, or even guards, or displeased because they were not appointed.

In the case of each delegate there may also be other men in attendance at the convention to whom he looks for advice or to whose suggestions he responds. His general chairman would probably be the most important of these, particularly to a delegate who is a local chairman. Field supervisors and state legislative representatives would also be influential, the former particularly with lodge treasurers and insurance representatives and the latter with local legislative representatives. All of these men, besides being influential with delegates from their area due to their personality and experience, might be able to help an ambitious delegate obtain a future appointment; and the general chairman might have small amounts of patronage at his own disposal for which local chairmen on his road might be grateful or hopeful. Since a number of general chairmen might be political opponents of the president, all the lines of patronage influence do not necessarily run in the same direction.

The delegates from the one hundred and twenty-six Canadian lodges regularly meet in caucus to propose a slate of candidates for the Canadian Grand Lodge positions, which now include two vice presidents, an alternate vice president, the Canadian legislative representative and an alternate, a member each of the Board of Trustees and Insurance, the Board of Trustees, and the Executive Board, and an alternate to the Board of Appeals. In making up the slate the delegates try to achieve a balance among the regions of Canada, with consideration to both the English and the French speaking areas, and to the employees of the two major railway systems. Since many rules in western Canada differ from those in the eastern part of the country, it is important to have Grand Lodge officers who are familiar with each area. Within the caucus there is a tendency for a man to respond to the suggestions of others that he would make a good candidate, rather than to promote his own candidacy, as is likely to be the case among delegates from the United States.

Once the caucus agrees upon a slate of candidates for the Canadian offices, cards with the entire group of names are printed and distributed among all the delegates to the convention. Men who have been considered but not selected by the caucus may, nevertheless, become candidates in the convention; this is recognized as their right, though there is some feeling that such behavior is "not cricket." Usually the caucus choice is elected by the convention, though occasionally, as at the 1954 convention, the candidate with caucus backing may be defeated by a rival candidate. Such cases are most likely to occur when there is a sharp division within the caucus, and when the candidate who runs without caucus support is a good speaker who creates a very favorable impression upon the delegates from the United States.

There is considerable resentment among the Canadian delegates when a Canadian officer not of their choice is elected by the convention. When a vice president was so elected in 1954, a resolution was introduced, bearing the signatures of seventy-seven Canadian delegates, complaining that a vice president had been "foisted" upon them by action of the American delegates and that their membership was being "dictated to." "The majority of Canadian delegates," the resolution stated, "strongly resent the lack of good will, faith and understanding manifest in this election." Pointing out that the successful candidate's lack of experience on the two major Canadian rail systems invited raiding, the resolution asked the president to assign only experienced and qualified officers to handle wage-rule and other important matters affecting the entire Canadian membership.[8]

Though agreement upon a slate for the Canadian Grand Lodge vacancies is its main business, the Canadian caucus may also consider other matters. Thus Canadian problems such as working conditions or pensions may be discussed and resolutions dealing with these matters sponsored in the convention, though individual delegates or groups of delegates may introduce such resolutions without first presenting them to the caucus. Or a delegate from the United States who is a candidate for Grand Lodge office may ask to appear before the Canadian caucus, which would allow him to do so without taking a position as a group on his or any other non-Canadian candidacy.

Issues at the 1960 Convention

Though the Brotherhood has had its share of internal political conflict in the past, the cleavage between rival groups has seldom, if ever, been greater than was true at the 1960 convention. There the dissatisfaction was more acute, the criticism more bitter, and the split deeper than in the past. For the first time in the union's history an organized political grouping retained its identity after the adjournment of the convention, seeking to recruit members for another test of strength at the following convention.

As the 1960 convention opened, the insurgent group charged that a special rather than a regular convention had been called to prevent a change in the age limitation, and that the 1954 delegates were used because, now six years older than when they had been elected, they would presumably be more sympathetic to aging Grand Lodge officers. In attacking the administration for using the 1954 convention delegates, however, the insurgent group was treading on dangerous ground, for it was challenging the selection of delegates to whom it had to appeal, at the same time, for votes. Possibly the legality of the convention could have been contested by court action on this ground, but at the risk of alienating large numbers of delegates whose support the insurgents hoped to win. The antiadministration group, therefore, accepted the delegates and appealed for their support in the key votes to come.

The first two test votes were won by the antiadministration group. One was to declare the convention a regular rather than a special convention, though for reasons already suggested this proposal was popular with many administration supporters as well. In the other vote an insurgent candidate, C. M. Wilkinson, was chosen over an administration leader, Assistant to the President V. W. Satterwhite, to chair the Committee of the Whole, by the narrow margin of 531 to 516.[9] Everyone knew that at this time there was a very large number of uncommitted delegates, and major attention was devoted by both groups to winning these delegates to their side. Efforts by the antiadministration group to send home any field supervisors, deputy presidents, or organizers who were receiving Grand Lodge pay while attending the convention, and to limit the pay of guards to the periods they were on duty, showed the fear of the insurgents of the influence that the administration could exert.

Though the insurgent group had seemed to be in control of the convention during the opening week, by the middle of the second week it was apparent that the balance of power had shifted to the administration forces. Even during the first week, the antiadministration group had lost an effort to amend the constitution to require the president and the assistant to the president to reside in Cleveland and spend at least one hundred days per year in that office.[10] This proposal, an obvious attack on Kennedy for spending so much time in Minneapolis, may have seemed to many delegates an effort unduly to limit the power of the president to spend his time wherever, in his judgment, the interests of the union were best served.

On January 14, the ninth day the convention met, the Committee of the Whole took up the crucial Section 8 of the constitution, dealing with the privileges and qualifications of Grand Lodge officers. A provision limiting the age of Grand Lodge officers had first became a convention issue in 1946, urged by anti-Whitney delegates who hoped by this means to compel Whitney, who had already passed seventy, to retire. The issue did not come to a vote then, however, and in 1954 the constitution was amended to provide that no one who had reached the age of seventy would be eligible to be elected or appointed a Grand Lodge officer or board member. As Kennedy's age advanced—he became sixty-five in 1957—his opponents hoped to force his retirement and also to open up a number of other positions, by reducing the age for eligibility to office from seventy to sixty-five.

When the Committee of the Whole reached Section 8 in 1960, the insurgent group offered a motion to reduce the eligibility age from seventy to sixty-five; this proposal was lost by a vote of 627 to 418. An effort to remove the age limitation altogether also went down to defeat. Thereupon a compromise proposal was introduced, under which the eligibility age would be reduced gradually, until it reached sixty-five after the calendar year 1964; after clarifying changes, this was adopted unanimously. Under the new constitutional provision, Kennedy would not be eligible to serve beyond December 31, 1962.[11] The sliding scale that was adopted had precedents, both in the action taken by another railroad union with regard to its officers, and in agreements negotiated by Brotherhood committees with leading carriers.

Another issue which showed the administration group to be firmly in control of the convention was the vote on a motion to sever immediately all connections with Attorney Ray T. Miller and not employ his law firm under any circumstances. Miller, a former mayor of Cleveland and a powerful Democratic leader in Cuyahoga County, had been charged by the heads of the Cleveland Federation of Labor with helping to raise funds for a "right-to-work" law campaign in Ohio. Miller, whose retention was urged by Kennedy, denied the charge. Despite the emotional appeal of such an issue to a union convention, the resolution was defeated, 527 to 467, in a standing vote, and again in a secret ballot vote by 555 to 508.[12]

The insurgent group was not wholly without victories, however, after the first week had passed. In the Committee of the Whole there was a long debate on a proposed amendment to Section 9 of the constitution, dealing with the duties of the president. Whereas the president until then had been empowered to suspend or remove a subordinate lodge officer for sufficient cause and to ban him from representing the union in any capacity, the

Constitution Committee now proposed that the president be authorized to disqualify the removed officer from holding any Brotherhood office for a period up to four years, which disqualification might be renewed for an additional period not to exceed the time in the original order. Instead a substitute was adopted, stating that the president was not empowered to remove a subordinate lodge official except when he was charged with violating the constitution or his duty as an officer, and not until he had had a fair trial in his own lodge.[13]

As an aftermath to Kennedy's revocation of Lodge 219's charter and his rulings which almost closed the avenues of legal communication among lodges, Section 144 was amended so that general circulars no longer required the president's approval; however, any member convicted of circulating untrue statements was to be expelled.[14] The portion of Section 132 which prohibited, on penalty of expulsion, the circulation of reports liable to cause trouble or injury to the Brotherhood was amended to punish only the circulation of untrue reports.[15]

The balloting for officers, which began on February 4, found the administration group solidly in control. Kennedy defeated Weil for the presidency by a vote of 641 to 464, with nine votes going to a third candidate. This margin, with variations according to the ability or popularity of the various candidates, was to hold roughly throughout the balloting. The contest for the assistant to the president, who under the new rules was to succeed automatically to the presidency on Kennedy's retirement at the end of 1962, found three candidates in the field—Charles Luna, Weil, and V. W. Satterwhite, the incumbent; both Luna and Satterwhite were administration supporters. The first ballot showed 488 for Luna, 486 for Weil, and 138 for Satterwhite. Satterwhite's name was then dropped, whereupon Luna was elected over Weil by a vote of 602 to 494.[16] Luna was widely credited with having organized the administration supporters into a bloc that effectively controlled the convention after the opening days; a vice president since 1954 and a general chairman on the Santa Fe before that, he had had considerable experience in collective bargaining and had won friends and supporters throughout the country.

Weil then ran for his old post as general secretary and treasurer, only to be defeated by the administration candidate, W. E.

B. Chase, 585 to 523. Weil made a fourth try, for the post of first vice president, but was defeated by the incumbent, B. W. Fern, 553 to 537. Weil now waited until the eleventh vice presidency was reached, and was elected to that position over F. C. Montgomery, an administration supporter, by a vote of 664 to 433. In the meantime several able and popular incumbents had been reelected vice presidents without opposition; in other cases the insurgent group put up candidates, who lost regularly by margins that ranged from 100 to over 400 votes, depending upon the appeal of particular candidates. It was apparent that the administration had a bloc of votes, 200 to 300 more than the insurgents could command, upon which they could usually count. Elections of alternate vice presidents followed the same pattern, as did the contests for membership on the various boards.

In one important respect the convention differed from past sessions in the long experience of the Brotherhood. While there had been spirited election contests in the past, the lines had remained relatively fluid, and a candidate defeated for a top position could usually count on a number of votes, cast against him for that office, swinging over to him if he ran for a lesser post. This time, however, factional lines had been drawn more sharply, the attack on the administration had been more sustained and bitter, and few delegates had remained neutral in the fight. Consequently, except for Weil's election to one of the lower vice presidencies, factional lines held to a degree never before approached in the union's history.

The bitterness aroused during the long preconvention struggle and during the many clashes at the convention was shown again on the final two days of the convention. On December 22, 1959, just a few days before the convention met, Lodge 909 of Boston, Massachusetts, had appealed to the Board of Directors from Kennedy's calling of the 1954 delegates to the convention, this being alleged to violate the Labor-Management Reporting and Disclosure Act of 1959. The Board of Directors, meeting two days before the convention opened, had denied the appeal, which was then taken to the convention's Committee on Appeals. The union's general counsel, in a discussion of this point to the convention, had expressed the opinion that no violation of the federal law had been committed by the use of the 1954 delegates. On February 17 the Committee on Appeals, concluding that neither the federal law nor the union's constitution had been violated, recommended that the appeal be denied, and the convention then tabled the appeal. On the following day, the final one of the convention, a motion to take the appeal from the table and take action upon it was lost. Two hundred and eleven delegates thereupon placed themselves on record as opposed to the committee's recommendation, and 244 delegates as opposed to the tabling of the appeal.[17]

In another last-day development a motion was offered to have the Brotherhood and its Insurance Department sue the members of the Board of Directors as individuals and any other persons to force the repayment of money illegally expended in calling the convention without electing delegates, and in spending large sums for field supervisors, organizers, excess guards, and excess election committeemen to promote Kennedy's candidacy. When the motion was lost, 210 delegates listed themselves as favoring the suit if the convention proved to be illegal.[18]

The factors that attracted delegates to the one camp or the other seem fairly clear, in most cases. The administration supporters were delegates who were satisfied with Kennedy's leadership, who were repelled by the tactics of the insurgent group, or who disliked dissension within the union. The internal dispute seemed to some just an effort on the part of a young and ambitious group, using questionable tactics, to win control of the union for personal gain. The insurgent group, on the other hand, included delegates who wanted a more aggressive program to deal with the economic problems facing the union, who were dissatisfied with Kennedy's leadership, or who were resentful because of the convention postponement. Some had been antagonized by various of the decisions that Kennedy had made over his years in the presidency, and hoped to use this opportunity to even old scores.

Weil's support came largely from the East, though he also enjoyed a following in the Midwest and far West; the South, by way of contrast, gave almost solid support to the administration. Most Canadian delegates also supported Kennedy, who had been born in the Dominion and who maintained close contacts there. Some of the administration supporters had great respect for Weil's ability, but thought that he should have waited until Kennedy's retirement before seeking the presidency. Though there were a number of general chairmen in the insurgent group, most of the influential general chairmen were supporters of the administration. There was an undercurrent of comment on the religious issue, since Kennedy was a Protestant and Weil a Catholic; though the support each received seemed to disregard religious lines, it is possible that some delegates were swayed, at least in part, by this difference between the candidates.

Since the elections were by voting machines, one cannot compare the size of the membership whose delegates voted for each camp. Indeed, since most delegates had been elected in 1953, before the issues that divided the convention arose, one cannot know the extent to which delegates represented the desires of their lodges in the election. Yet there was a widespread belief that most of the delegates from the large lodges in the East and some in the Midwest voted for Weil, whereas smaller lodges in the West and South supported the administration. There may be a tendency in any labor organization for small locals to be more favorable to the administration, simply because they are more dependent upon outside help, as well as more isolated. Large locals, on the other hand, are somewhat more likely to develop their own leadership and to advance their own programs for the solution of national as well as local problems.

Before the delegates left for home, the insurgent group made plans for an organization to continue its struggle within the union. Called the 460 Club, after the vote that they had registered at the convention, the group planned to enroll members and issue a monthly letter, looking toward a renewal of the fight at the next convention. How successful they would be, once the issue of avoiding a convention was no longer available to them, remained to be seen. In view of the compulsory retirement of Kennedy at the end of 1962 and the succession of Luna to the presidency, it was also a question whether, or to what extent, the alignment of 1960 would persist. It also remained for the future to show whether this development, which on the whole separated the younger and more aggressive members from the older and more conservative ones, could mark the beginning of a permanent factional alignment within the union.

9

The Political Spirit of the Union

In the foregoing chapters the account of the experience of the Brotherhood makes it apparent that there is a strong democratic tradition in the life of the union. This is shown by the repeated and vigorous contests for office, at the highest as well as at the lower levels of the organization, and by the tendency of the delegates to elect the candidate whom they defeated for the presidency to another national office, thereby preserving his leadership of the antiadministration group and enabling him to renew the contest, if he so wishes, at succeeding conventions. Thus Whitney was able to remain in a strong challenging position despite his repeated defeats in his campaigns for the presidency, and Lee, when he finally lost the president's office, was kept in the Grand Lodge as general secretary and treasurer. In many other unions, by way of contrast, the defeated candidate for the presidency finds no union post of importance open to him, and often runs the risk of expulsion for dual unionism or for statements made in the heat of the campaign.

The 1960 convention showed that the democratic tradition within the union remained as strong as ever. The organization of an opposition group prior to the convention, its repeated circularization of the lodges, the public meetings of delegates sponsored by various groups at the convention, the distribution of literature dealing with union issues and candidates for office, and the formation of the 460 Club, following the convention, to continue the internal struggle all bore witness to the democratic structure and practices of the union. This is not meant to indicate approval of any of these actions, but rather of the union tradition that made them possible. No efforts were made to discipline opposition groups simply for forming,[1] whereas in many unions charges would have been filed against them for dual unionism, with expulsion the likely penalty.

The conduct of the elections at the 1960 convention also bore testimony to the union's democratic practices. There was no suspicion of dishonesty in the count; indeed, with voting machines employed, candidates' watchers permitted, and a large committee supervising their use, the balloting was conducted in exemplary fashion. It was evidence of and a tribute to the union's democratic traditions that a leading officer like Weil, after his unsuccessful campaign for the presidency, with all the bitterness that that contest aroused, could increase his votes for several other leading positions before finally being elected to one of the lower-ranking vice presidencies.

Within the administration group, at the 1960 convention as at earlier ones, two or more candidates were at liberty to contest the same office, with the candidate showing the greater appeal to the delegates elected to the office by the united proadministration vote after the other had been eliminated. Often in other unions the key political figure selects the slate that will run with him, with the delegates' function being merely to ratify his choice.

Even the way in which subordinate lodges communicate with their national officers is evidence of a spirit of independence within the ranks of the union. In motions that are adopted in the local lodges asking the national heads for information or for their position on some issue there are occasional references to the fact that the officers are elected and paid their salaries by the membership, and this is said just as bluntly in the letters sent the officers following the lodge meetings. A lodge may send a separate letter to each Grand Lodge officer, asking him to state his position on a controversial issue.

Perhaps an illustration may be given here of the manner in which local officers sometimes write to the national heads of the union. In 1956 Lodge 229, dissatisfied with some changes in the agreement negotiated with the carrier by a subgeneral committee and a deputy president, appealed to Kennedy. Finding his answer unsatisfactory, in that it did not say clearly enough for their understanding whether the appeal was upheld or denied, the secretary-treasurer of the lodge wrote to Kennedy again, stating in part:

It is apparent, recently, that there is less consideration being given to the rights of the members, granted by the Constitution, by general chairmen on various railways and Grand Lodge officers negotiating agreements without receiving the proper authority required by the Constitution.

We do not want this organization to drift toward dictatorship in any sense of the word.

Action was taken by the lodge at the regular meeting held May 14, 1956, that I write to you and endeavor to clarify some of the questions . . . and also to demand a definite answer as to whether the appeal is upheld or denied.[2]

In his reply, without commenting on the wording or tone of the secretary-treasurer's communication, Kennedy referred to the final paragraph of his earlier letter, which indicated clearly, he said, that under the circumstances he had no alternative other than to deny the appeal. Although the president of the Brotherhood has substantial powers with regard to appeals, it is clear that the membership feels free to state its position vigorously. The literature that is distributed at conventions by groups of delegates or by individual members of the union, samples of which have been given earlier, is testimony to the same attitude.

The tradition of a vigorous, independent spirit on the part of Brotherhood members, it is evident, has long persisted. More than that, the union under Kennedy clearly has been a more democratic institution than under Whitney, whereas the general tendency for national unions has been to move in the reverse direction as the years go by. A comparison of the ways in which Whitney and Kennedy used their powers shows what a difference personality makes, even though the basic constitutional framework under which the two presidents operated remained fundamentally the same. Primarily, except for his efforts to postpone the convention, Kennedy has exercised his powers with moderation, whereas Whitney sought to drive out of office various officers who balked his will.

Yet under both presidents there was a high degree of loyalty on the part of the general membership to the organization, a reflection of the fact that the Brotherhood has consistently promoted the interests of the members in collective bargaining negotiations, in grievance handling, and in legislative and insurance matters. Had either president failed to satisfy the basic desires of the membership for effective representation in the employment relationship, he would have gone down to defeat at the hands of one of the rival candidates for the presidency, usually available at a Brotherhood convention.

The earlier discussion of the ways in which recent presidents of the Brotherhood have used their authority has shown that, while a vigorous union head exercises substantial power, he cannot act in too arbitrary a fashion without creating dissatisfaction and setting in motion forces that might lead to his defeat. A study such as this, which focuses attention upon the political life of the union, is apt to spotlight precisely those acts of a president in which, challenged and perhaps angry, he deals with threats to his position. If he loses his patience or his judgment in any aspect of his work, he is most likely to do so here. Yet the test of freedom within a union, as in almost any other type of organization, is what happens to the dissenter, and how the leading official uses his power, such as in the area of discipline, to deal with critics and challengers. It is the administration that possesses power, and, therefore, it is the administration that must guard against its abuse, making a record that can withstand scrutiny.

Factors Inhibiting Political Opposition

Despite the factors that have been referred to as evidence of an unusually strong democratic spirit within the Brotherhood, the national president of the organization has a substantial array of powers, plus other perquisites, that give him a strong hold on his office and that tend to discourage political opposition. Many of these advantages are common to the presidencies of national unions generally—or indeed, to the top positions in many other types of organizations as well—whereas several are unusual, in or out of the labor movement.

Among the factors that are found generally in the labor movement are the president's advantage in publicity, his control over avenues of communication within the union, his patronage powers, and his part in the disciplinary process. From the national office of the Brotherhood a steady stream of letters, circulars, and reports goes to the subordinate lodges, almost all of it in the name of the president. His name and picture appear in the daily press as well, in connection with negotiations with the carriers, legislation in which the union is interested, or important developments within the Brotherhood. Other public channels of communication—news magazines, radio, and television—likewise take account of his doings. Better still, the union's weekly newspaper, whose editor he appoints, functions in part as a personal organ, featuring his activities, recording his achievements, and presenting him always in the best possible light. News developments critical of the president seldom, if ever, are mentioned in the paper. His constitutional duty to "supervise the Official Publication" give him an enormous political advantage over any possible opponent, by carrying favorable publicity, week after week, into the home of every member of the union. It is impossible for any opposition candidate to match this steady stream of favorable publicity, and any effort to offset it even to a small degree entails tremendous effort and expense.

Until 1960, moreover, the president had the power to block the distribution of general circulars throughout the union simply by withholding his approval, and to discipline lodges or individuals who distributed material in defiance of his authority. This power, together with control of the union newspaper, could be used to block the channels of communication for dissident groups within the union. The 1960 convention, however, changed the constitution to permit circularization, without need for approval, so long as the statements were true. This was a desirable change, since effective democracy requires the right to issue circulars, as to communicate in other ways; the cause of democracy is best served, however, where only truthful statements are made, and where the party making the statements signs them so that responsibility is clearly established.

The president adds to the advantages discussed above by his

constant travel about the country, and his appearances before as many of the active members as possible, at local or state meetings and on ceremonial or festive occasions. All of this activity, though it deals with union problems and not with his political fortunes, is the best possible political campaigning; and the expense of all of it, like the cost of the newspaper, is borne, and properly so, by the union treasury.

In addition the president has substantial patronage powers at his disposal. Besides filling positions at national headquarters, he may appoint deputy presidents and organizers as he finds necessary. The incessant efforts to win bargaining rights from other unions, as well as to defend the Brotherhood from raids and to organize in new territory, call for the appointment of organizers at the discretion of the president. The power to appoint perhaps dozens of deputy presidents and from one to two thousand organizers each year, for varying periods of time, adds up to enormous political power. In addition the president is usually influential in the election of other Grand Lodge officers, even though, as we have seen, the delegates show an unusually high degree of independence in this respect. The president's power to assign duties and territories to the vice presidents increases his control over them.

Even though an organizer may be on the payroll for only a few days, his appointment is recognition for which he is grateful; as a result he probably feels obligated and sympathetic to the president, and inclined to vote for re-election. The practice of keeping skeletal lodges alive after bargaining rights have been lost helps to perpetuate a president in office, if the men whom he appoints as organizers when the representation issue is timely are also the delegates to the convention. Even appointments to convention committees and as guards, with the very limited payments that these involve, are believed, as the preceding discussion has shown, to exert some influence over the voting behavior of the recipients.

There are two additional patronage networks, seldom found in other unions, at the disposal of the president of the Brotherhood. One is the power to appoint field supervisors, usually about fifty in number, to take charge of the sale and servicing of insurance policies. Field supervisors are usually in attendance at conventions, though they have no required duties there. To the extent that they are influential with the delegates from the lodges they serve—and this is particularly likely to be the case if the delegate is an insurance representative—they serve as a means of influence, subject to the president's control, operating outside of the normal political channels of the union. Along with this there are the legal aid representatives, also appointed by the president. There is a widespread belief within the union that both the field supervisors and the lawyers, dependent upon the president for their profitable professional connections or businesses, may help to serve the political purposes and promote the political interests of the president.

To all of this must be added the important part that the president plays in the disciplinary procedure within the union. Whitney made this a weapon of great power, by his tendency to file charges against Grand Lodge officers who displeased him, and by his removal of local officers, whom he often banned for indefinite periods from representing the Brotherhood in any capacity. The president's power to discipline local officers has been limited, both by the Labor-Management Reporting and Disclosure Act of 1959 and by changes made in the union's constitution in 1960. Three boards share authority in disciplinary cases, the Executive Board with regard to charges filed against Grand Lodge officers, and the Board of Directors and the Board of Appeals in cases of discipline involving other union officers or members. With regard to these three boards, therefore, the crucial question is whether they are subservient to the president's will. Earlier chapters have suggested that the Board of Directors, because of its composition, may function as an imperfect check upon the president, and that in the past the president on occasion exerted great influence over the other two boards, both of which functioned on a part-time basis, by appointing their members to other Grand Lodge positions in the interim periods.

The union now seeks to preserve the independence of these two boards, so necessary if the disciplinary procedures of the union are to operate fairly, by making the members ineligible to hold any other Grand Lodge office during the period of service on either board. While this provision is of great help, one must also recognize that members of the two boards may feel indebted to the president for their election, or hopeful for his support should they become candidates for full-time Grand Lodge posts. An independent judiciary to review discipline cases has yet to be achieved by the Brotherhood. Its procedure in this respect, however, is superior to that of the many unions that have their general executive boards function as appeal agencies, though inferior to the practice of the very small number of unions that have established outside review boards.

In addition to his power to discipline local lodge officers, the president has rather broad authority to revoke the charters of subordinate lodges, though there has been little abuse of this power in the history of the Brotherhood. The subordinate lodge, indeed, is more firmly under the authority of the national union organization than is true in the American labor movement generally. There, until the no-raiding agreements of recent years, a dissatisfied local could affiliate with another union, at times in a rival federation, so long as it could retain control over its bargaining rights and, therefore, assure jobs to its members. If no rival union was available, it could function as an independent local union, provided it could win an election and obtain National Labor Relations Board certification. This is not the case under the Railway Labor Act, where bargaining rights, as well as representation on the Adjustment Board, are limited to organizations national in scope.

Nor can the subordinate lodge get very far in its bargaining and grievance work without the cooperation of higher union authorities. The local chairman cannot go above the carrier's superintendent, requiring the intervention of the general chairman before an issue may be carried higher within the management structure. Due to the nature of competition in the industry, moreover, the general level of wages and many of the most important rules changes must be handled in national negotiations, which the president of the Brotherhood controls. Yet the president must use his very considerable authority in the collective bargaining sphere so as to retain the support of general chairmen and other key officials, and likewise satisfy the membership that their interests are being promoted to the greatest possible extent. Let the membership become dissatisfied with the administration's record in collective bargaining, and opposition political groups will develop or secession movements occur.

Factors Encouraging Political Independence

This array of powers and advantages possessed by the president seems formidable enough; yet the persistently democratic traditions of the union show that they must be counterbalanced by forces working in the opposite direction. Among these forces the railroader's job security, the communications advantages enjoyed by the Brotherhood members, the homogeneity of the membership, the existence of satisfying union jobs not controlled by the national office, the diffusion of power within the Grand Lodge, the independence of convention delegates, and the existence of state insurance authorities with jurisdiction over an important part of the union's work all play a part.

Among these many factors one of the most significant is the sense of job security that the member of the Brotherhood enjoys. Once a man has a few years of seniority, he tends to remain for life, not merely in the industry, but with the same company and on the same yard or district seniority roster. The sharp decline in recent years in railroad employment has altered this situation, though almost all of the men who are active in the union have enough seniority to be protected against lay-offs when the volume of traffic is low. Even bankruptcy probably means merely that another management group will continue operations. After one has held union office, a return to work on the railroads is not too undesirable; by that time one is probably near the top of the seniority list, enjoying one's pick of the assignments available. Nor is expulsion from the union the serious penalty that it is in many other fields. The expelled worker may retain his insurance, and he keeps his job, even where a union shop clause is in effect, by tendering dues or by joining a rival union, if one is available for his classification in his area.

In the course of their work, moreover, the members are in constant communication with each other, and also with the yard crews of neighboring carriers, who may or may not belong to the same lodge. News travels quickly under such circumstances, and dissatisfaction, similarly, can be translated relatively easily into an organized movement. This is a far different situation from that which exists in a union whose members work in isolated localities, with a union business agent and perhaps a union paper serving as the principal channels of communication between local meetings. Local switching associations and state or area meetings help this process of communication among leading officers of the various lodges.

Communication and organization are facilitated by the homogeneity of the union membership. There is almost no difference in educational level, and little difference in duties or base pay save those that seniority brings to each group of men in turn. Organized into relatively small lodges with stable, long-term memberships, the men know each other and their officers personally, and learn their rights under the complex set of rules that governs employment in the industry.

The conflicts of interest, actual or potential, that exist between roadmen and yardmen or between conductors and brakemen are of less significance than the interests they have in common. The same is true of sectional differences, and of differences between those living in metropolitan areas as against those living in small towns. Where the membership is not divided into rival pressure groups by skill, level of pay, race, national origin, or some other factor, it is more likely that any effort by officers to infringe upon the democratic rights of some will meet with criticism and opposition from nearly all.

In this union an ambitious member is not dependent upon administration favor for an opportunity to learn leadership skills and obtain satisfying union posts. Within each subordinate lodge there is a local chairman for each seniority district, elected by the men in that district, to handle grievances with management; and on each carrier there is a general chairman, elected by the local chairmen or by referendum vote of the membership, to settle the stubborn grievances with top management. The local chairman's position is a training ground for the post of general chairman, as the local legislative representative's job is for that of state legislative representative.

The position of general chairman is a full-time one on a road of substantial size, carrying with it an attractive salary, satisfying authority and duties, and a chance to build a record of achievement that makes one a serious contender for Grand Lodge office. In the meantime one develops leadership skills and acquires a political base as one services the local lodges, wins their confidence, and earns their gratitude. A general chairman even has a limited amount of patronage, that very important political asset, available to him. A state legislative representative likewise holds a desirable and satisfying job that is beyond the control of the national office. One who holds an office such as either of these may disagree freely with the national officers without suffering a penalty, so long as he does a good job for his membership and continues to receive their support. Similarly, one who loses Grand Lodge office may have to go back to work in the yards or on the trains only temporarily, before becoming a candidate for one of these posts.

Within the Grand Lodge, in addition, authority is diffused more than in most unions, even though very substantial powers, as we have seen, are vested in the president. Though the position of vice president is weakened by convention-wide election, by subjection to the direction of the president, and by dependence upon him for the assignment of duties and territory, this is counterbalanced by the existence of a large number of boards, each with an important place in the union's functioning and in its structure of authority. Particularly important, from this point of view, are the Executive Board, which investigates charges against Grand Lodge officers, and the Board of Appeals, the most important group in the disciplinary procedure; since members of these boards, neither of which offers a full-time post, are not permitted to hold other Grand Lodge office, rank-and-file influence makes itself felt in important places within the Grand Lodge structure. This influence is weakened, however, to the extent that members of these boards hope, by currying favor with the president, to obtain his support for full-time Grand Lodge positions in the future.

Though the degree of independence of these boards, and likewise of the Board of Directors, may be limited, in other respects the appeals machinery of the Brotherhood is admirable. Any action of a subordinate lodge or of a general committee is subject to appeal, both from the point of view of procedure and of substance. At every step in the appeals procedure, which on many issues leads finally to the convention, due process is protected; the views of all parties of interest are obtained, the written statements filed by one party are made available to others, and all interested persons have the right to appear personally to present their arguments. If greater efforts were made to assure an impartial and independent judiciary, the appeals mechanism of the Brotherhood would be exemplary.

Still another factor is the power of the convention and the independence of convention delegates. The convention is the Grand Lodge, which has supreme authority within the Brotherhood; the unhurried pace of its sessions tends to leave authority in the hands of the delegates to a much greater extent than is true in most unions, where the convention often seems to function as a demonstration and an agency to ratify policies decided elsewhere rather than as a serious policy-making assembly. When conventions last for from five to seven weeks, as with the Brotherhood, there is ample time for delegates to become informed on issues, and sufficient opportunity for them to express their opinions and seek to convert others to their views. Many of the delegates, moreover, have become skilled in debate with railroad officials; the importance of precedent in grievances makes amateur lawyers of them all, experience that stands them in good stead in convention debate.

Though a number of the delegates may be indebted to the president for past appointments or may hope for such favors in the future, patronage considerations can hardly sway a majority of the 1,100 delegates in attendance at a convention. Others may be influenced by field supervisors, general chairmen, state legislative representatives, or other officials, though there is always the chance that pressure of this sort may be resented and may harm the cause in which it is exerted; and general chairmen and state legislative representatives may use their influence either in a proadministration or in an antiadministration direction. While officials who deal with insurance, grievances, and legislation have friends in the lodges they service with whom they may be influential, they are also dependent upon these friends for cooperation in the sale of policies, in the case of the field supervisor, or for support, upon the expiration of their terms, in the cases of the general chairman and the state legislative representative. Field supervisors, who hold office by appointment of the president, seldom dare to oppose him; general chairmen and state legislative representatives may be free agents politically, however, so long as they enjoy such solid support among the groups they represent that the president's influence is unable to defeat them.

All of this means that the administration's influence upon delegates, while important, is nevertheless limited; it may provide the margin of votes essential to victory in a reasonably close contest, but it cannot reach the point of complete machine domination. As against this there is the enormous cost of conventions, two and a half to three million dollars in recent years. While democracy is worth its necessary cost, this is an enormous price for a membership of under two hundred thousand to pay every fourth year; ways might well be found for shortening conventions and thereby reducing the expense without sacrificing the essential contribution of the convention to democratic control.

Also important, from the point of view of democracy, is the practice in conventions of electing one officer at a time, and likewise the tradition of permitting a candidate who is defeated for one office to run for a lesser one without loss of prestige. The value of this is that it keeps opposing leaders in high posts where they are in a position to watch each other's actions, rally their followers, and renew the contest at the following convention. In too many other unions, by way of contrast, a candidate defeated for the presidency would face the alternatives of returning to his old job in the industry or leaving the union; often he chooses the latter course, leaving the victorious candidate and his allies in undisputed control.

Added to all these factors is the existence, as a result of the insurance activity of the Brotherhood, of the state insurance laws that regulate the union's Insurance Department, and of state insurance commissioners as independent regulatory authorities to whom appeal may be made on some issues. Certainly this proved to be an important factor in the long controversy over the calling of the convention that assembled early in 1960. Whereas in most unions a dissatisfied group may constitute itself a political opposition within the union, file court action in certain types of situations, and as a last resort join or form a rival union, in the case of the Brotherhood there is the additional weapon, in appropriate cases, of appeal to the state insurance officials. The Labor-Management Reporting and Disclosure Act of 1959 provides additional rights to union members, railroad workers as well as others.

To this list of objective factors that have encouraged the development of a democratic tradition within the Brotherhood must be added the force of that tradition itself, which has shown toughness and resiliency throughout the union's long history, and which forms an important part of the environment in which the future leaders of the union are trained. The tradition strengthens and legitimatizes the democratic practices that the objective conditions permit. Whether the practices could long survive in the absence of the objective conditions encouraging them is highly doubtful; but the objective conditions and the tradition, reinforcing each other, give encouragement that the democratic practices of the union will continue far into the future.

Footnotes

CHAPTER 1

1. *Proceedings of the Thirty-first Convention of the Brotherhood of Railroad Trainmen,* 1960, pp. 298–299.
2. These figures were computed by the Railway Labor Executives' Association from reports of the Interstate Commerce Commission. See testimony of H. E. Gilbert, president of the Brotherhood of Locomotive Firemen and Enginemen, *Hearings before the Subcommittee on Surface Transportation of the Committee on Interstate and Foreign Commerce, United States Senate, Eighty-fifth Congress, Second Session, on Problems of the Railroads,* 1958, Part 4, p. 2183. Averages were computed by dividing the total compensation paid each group of employees, including all straight time, overtime, vacation pay, and other constructive allowances, by the average number of employees on the payroll.
3. On the characteristics of switching as an occupation, see an unpublished M.A. paper by Duane Beeler, *The Railroad Switchman* (1960), in the University of Chicago library. The general characteristics of railroad workers are discussed in W. Fred Cottrell, *The Railroader* (Stanford University, California: Stanford University Press, 1940).
4. Walter F. McCaleb, *Brotherhood of Railroad Trainmen, with Special Reference to the Life of Alexander F. Whitney* (New York: Albert & Charles Boni, 1936), pp. 59, 125.
5. *Proceedings of the Thirtieth Convention,* 1954, pp. 227–228.
6. *Report of the President, 1958,* p. 86; *Report of the Board of Directors, 1958,* pp. 48–55.

7. The best accounts of railroad labor legislation and of collective bargaining experiences in the industry are to be found in Jacob J. Kaufman, *Collective Bargaining in the Railroad Industry* (New York: King's Crown Press, 1954); Leonard A. Lecht, *Experience under Railway Labor Legislation* (New York: Columbia University Press, 1955); Harry D. Wolf, "Railroads," in Harry A. Millis, editor, *How Collective Bargaining Works: A Survey of Experience in Leading American Industries* (New York: The Twentieth Century Fund, 1942), pp. 318–380; Harry E. Jones, *Railroad Wages and Labor Relations, 1900–1952* (no publisher listed, 1953); and P. Harvey Middleton, *Railways and Organized Labor* (Chicago: Railway Business Association, 1941).

8. *Report of W. P. Kennedy, President, Brotherhood of Railroad Trainmen, on 1949–51 Rules-Wage Movement in United States* (Cleveland: Brotherhood of Railroad Trainmen, no date), p. 83.

9. From 1939 to 1959 average gross weekly earnings on Class I railroads rose from $31.90 to $106.17, an increase of 332.8 per cent. In the same period the corresponding figure for manufacturing increased from $23.86 to $89.47, for a gain of 375 per cent. In average gross hourly earnings the railroad workers maintained a lead in absolute figures, earning 73 cents in 1939 to 63.3 cents for manufacturing workers, and $2.54 in 1959 as compared with $2.22 in manufacturing. In percentage terms manufacturing workers gained slightly more on an hourly basis over this period. See *Economic Report of the President Transmitted to the Congress January 20, 1960* (Washington: United States Government Printing Office, 1960), pp. 183–184.

10. For management's view of the work rules issue, see *Facts about Featherbedding in the Railway Industry* (Washington, D.C.: Association of American Railroads, pamphlet, no date); "Year of Decision: Clear Track or Crisis?" the address of Daniel P. Loomis, President of the Association of American Railroads, before the National Association of Shippers Advisory Boards in St. Louis, Feb. 11, 1959; and "The Work Rules Trap," *Railway Age*, March 24, 1958, pp. 18–23, 30–33. For the union view, see "The Truth about the Railroads," the address of G. E. Leighty, Chairman of the Railway Labor Executives' Association, before the Southeastern Association of Railroad and Utilities Commissioners at Miami Beach, Florida, April 16, 1959; and "Are Railroad Workers 'Featherbedding'?" an address by Eli Oliver to the Washington Chapter of the Industrial Relations Research Association, May 27, 1959. For an impartial view, see Kaufman, *op. cit.*, pp. 26–44. The most recent statement of the union position is in a pamphlet, *The Work-Rules Dispute*, issued in 1962 by the five operating brotherhoods.

11. Under the dual system of pay by time or miles, 100 miles was established as a full day's run in freight service and 150 miles in passenger service in 1919. Though the speed of trains has been substantially increased since then, the mileage definition of a basic day's work has remained unchanged. Management wants to change the definition of a basic day to 8 hours or 160 miles for through freight runs, and 8 hours or 240 miles in passenger service.

CHAPTER 2

1. For a case of this sort, see *Report of the Board of Directors, 1952,* pp. 49–52.

2. For a case of this sort, in which the president authorized formation of a new lodge, following investigation by and recommendations of a vice president, see *Report of the President, 1956,* p. 236.

3. For an unfavorable decision of this sort, upheld by the president of the Brotherhood on the grounds that the complaining group had thus far received satisfactory representation, see *Report of the President, 1959,* p. 76.

4. For such a request, with the solution referred to, see *Report of the President, 1954,* p. 251.

5. This case appears in *Report of the Board of Appeals, July, 1958,* pp. 9–14.

6. *Report of the Board of Appeals, January, 1957,* pp. 78–84.

7. *Report of the Board of Appeals, January, 1956,* pp. 360–372.

8. *Report of the President, 1956,* pp. 69–70; *Report of the Board of Directors, 1956,* pp. 60–64.

9. *Proceedings of the Sixth Triennial Convention,* 1931, pp. 469–470 and 483–484; *Proceedings of the Twenty-eighth Convention,* 1946, pp. 637–639; *Proceedings of the Thirtieth Convention,* 1954, pp. 384–385, 394–395, and 507–508.

10. This case is discussed in full in *Report of the Board of Appeals, July, 1957,* pp. 86–99.

11. See *Report of the President, 1958,* pp. 87–88. The paragraph quoted appears on page 88.

12. *Report of the Board of Directors, 1957,* pp. 51–53; *Report of the Board of Appeals, January, 1958,* pp. 246–252.

13. *Report of the Board of Appeals, January, 1956,* pp. 344–350.

14. For a case of this sort, see *Proceedings of the Twenty-ninth Convention,* 1950, pp. 429–433.

15. *Report of the President, 1958,* pp. 115–117. This recommendation, in which the president of the Brotherhood concurred, was disapproved on appeal by the Board of Appeals, on the grounds that the Grand Lodge officer had considered matters not properly before him, and that an offer by the Lines West general chairman to consolidate seniority lists should have been accepted. See *Report of the Board of Appeals, July, 1958,* pp. 96–152. For a further appeal and ruling in this case see *Report of the Board of Appeals, July, 1961,* pp. 16–50.

16. *Report of the President, 1955,* p. 79.

17. For a case of this sort, see *Report of the President, 1956, pp.* 152–153.

18. *Report of the President, 1959,* pp. 169–170.

19. *Report of the Board of Appeals, July, 1956,* pp. 606–622.

20. *Report of the Board of Appeals, January, 1956,* pp. 3–18; *Report of the Board of Appeals, July, 1956,* pp. 505–515.

21. *Report of the Board of Appeals, January, 1956,* pp. 99–109. For another case involving the same general principle, this time involving terminal work, see *Report of the Board of Directors, 1954,* pp. 58–67.
22. *Report of the Board of Appeals, January, 1956,* pp. 372–387. A similar case is described in *Report of the Board of Appeals, July, 1956,* pp. 865–879.
23. *Report of the President, 1959,* pp. 260–261.
24. Section 46 of the union's constitution lists the grounds for revocation of charters.

CHAPTER 3

1. For a case of this sort, involving a general chairman who was guilty of irregularities in the handling of his duties, see *Report of the Board of Directors, 1953,* pp. 26–29.
2. Brotherhood of Railroad Trainmen v. Chicago River & Indiana Railroad Co., 353 U.S. 30 (1957).
3. For a case in which a general chairman tried to organize a secession movement, following his removal from office by the president, see *Report of the President, 1947,* pp. 231–232 and 336–339.
4. *Proceedings of the International Association of General Chairmen, November 11 and 12, 1959,* pp. 2–13.

CHAPTER 4

1. *Report of the Board of Directors, 1957,* pp. 4–7 and 7–11. The quotation from the president's letter to the secretary of the lodge appears on p. 5.
2. *Report of the Board of Directors, 1954,* pp. 42–44.
3. President Kennedy's view, as stated to the author, is that the term "general circulation" meant a mailing to all the lodges in the union. He points out that general committees have always been able to circularize the lodges on their own systems without presidential approval, though on large roads as many as seventy-five to one hundred lodges were involved.
4. *Report of the President, 1959,* p. 49; *Proceedings of the Thirty-first Convention,* 1960, pp. 297 and 88–107. The number of days that each deputy president or organizer worked in these capacities during 1959 is given on pp. 88–107.

CHAPTER 5

1. See *Proceedings of the Third Triennial Convention,* 1922, pp. 302–305, 314, 630–640.
2. For a recital of the Lee-Whitney feud, told from Whitney's point of view, see McCaleb, *Brotherhood of Railroad Trainmen, with Special Reference*

to the Life of Alexander F. Whitney (New York: Albert & Charles Boni, 1936).

3. The letters are reproduced in H. Edens, *Enemies of Bill Lee and Foes of the Trainmen's Brotherhood* (Waco, Texas: Kelley-Bone Ptg. Co., no date), pp. 39–40 and 42–43.

4. For a laudatory account of Whitney and his leadership of the union, see McCaleb, *op. cit.;* for a sympathetic treatment, emphasizing his militancy in dealing with the carriers, see the chapter, "Alexander F. Whitney: The Railroads and the Brotherhoods," in Charles A. Madison, *American Labor Leaders: Personalities and Forces in the Labor Movement* (New York: Harper & Brothers, 1950), pp. 235–263; for a highly critical view, with considerable emphasis upon Whitney's dictatorial tendencies within the union, see Wellington Roe, *Juggernaut: American Labor in Action* (Philadelphia and New York: J. B. Lippincott Company, 1948), pp. 276–301.

5. For the discussion of the pressures on the union, and the amendment to the union's insurance rules as a result, see *Proceedings of the Twenty-eighth Convention,* 1946, pp. 727–729. The decision to use yellow paper appears on p. 663.

6. For the roll-call vote on Baumberger's appeal from the decision of the Executive Board, see *Proceedings of the Twenty-ninth Convention,* 1950, pp. 244–254. Kennedy's announcement on removing the restrictions appears on pp. 271–272. For the reports of the convention's Appeals Committee on the salary issue, see pp. 446–465. Whitney's account of the episode that precipitated the charges appears in *Report of the President, 1947,* pp. 344–354.

7. The circular and ballot are reproduced in *Report of the President,* 1956, pp. 55–58.

8. The pertinent portion of the letter, dated May 11, 1956, and addressed to William J. McCafferty, is reproduced in a pamphlet by Clyde Titler, *Our Fight for Democracy,* p. 12. The pamphlet was distributed among delegates to the 1960 convention.

9. Quoted in a letter from Weil to Kennedy, dated April 14, 1959. This letter, which was printed and widely distributed, reviewed developments up to that time in the fight over a convention.

10. *Ibid.*

11. The full text of the letter, and of a subsequent one sent by McHugh to all local lodge officers on May 27, are reproduced in a booklet, *The Underground Attack on the Brotherhood of Railroad Trainmen,* which was prepared by President Kennedy for the delegates to the Thirty-first Convention, which met in January, 1960. McHugh's first letter appears as Exhibit 4 and his second one as Exhibit 6.

12. This circular, plus all the other ones subsequently issued by the Committee of the Hundred, was reproduced in *The Underground Attack on the Brotherhood of Railroad Trainmen.*

13. The resolution appears in the monthly *Circular of Instructions,* Number 119, June, 1959. Other resolutions to the same effect appear in the *Circular of Instructions* for August, 1959.

14. The letter and press release are reproduced in the circular of the Committee of the Hundred, dated July 28, which in turn appears in *The Underground Attack on the Brotherhood of Railroad Trainmen*.
15. A summary of the decision appears in *Trainman News*, August 3, 1959.
16. The court's opinion is reproduced in full in *Proceedings of the Thirty-first Convention*, 1960, pp. 253–268.
17. The resolution of the Board of Directors is reproduced in *Report of the President, 1959*, pp. 51–52.
18. The letter is reproduced in *The Underground Attack on the Brotherhood of Railroad Trainmen* as Exhibit 3.

CHAPTER 6

1. For the motion that was adopted, see *Proceedings of the Thirtieth Convention*, 1954, p. 532, and for the results of the election, see pp. 544, 567–568. For the way in which they were listed, see subsequent issues of the *Directory of the Grand Lodge and Subordinate Lodges of the Brotherhood of Railroad Trainmen*, published quarterly.
2. The appeal is reported in *Proceedings of the Thirty-first Convention*, 1960, pp. 664–671. The decision of the Board of Directors denying the appeal was in turn appealed to the convention, which considered the issue on the thirty-third day—the day before adjournment—and voted to table the appeal.
3. For a case in which a second ballot was required, see *Report of the Board of Directors, 1951*, pp. 24–25. In that case sixteen candidates were nominated for a vacancy on the Executive Board, though only three received votes. For other cases in which the board split three ways on filling vacancies, see *Report of the Board of Directors, 1952*, p. 34, and *Report of the Board of Directors, 1953*, p. 65.
4. This case is reported in *Report of the Board of Directors, 1955*, pp. 43–44, and in *Proceedings of the Thirty-first Convention*, 1960, pp. 443–446. The resolution that gave rise to the controversy appears in *Proceedings of the Thirtieth Convention*, 1954, p. 337.
5. The telegrams are reproduced in *Trainmen's Views*, Jan. 23, 1960. This was a series of anonymous circulars, in a format modeled roughly on the union's newspaper, *Trainman News*, and distributed to the delegates to the 1960 convention in support of Weil's candidacy for the presidency. The title and format of *Trainmen's Views* were evidently calculated to appear to the hasty reader as issues of the union's official paper. Kennedy has stated to the author that he sent the telegrams in an effort to save union funds. The alternative on both occasions, in his view, would have been to convene the board in Cleveland for the election of the chairman, an expensive operation in view of the fact that board members lived in widely separated parts of the United States and Canada and had no other business to transact.

CHAPTER 7

1. See, for example, *Proceedings of the Twenty-ninth Convention*, 1950, p. 328, for a resolution signed by twenty-eight delegates protesting the fact that the editor of *Trainman News* and two of his assistants were non-members, although the constitution provided that preference in employment be given to Brotherhood members.
2. *Proceedings of the Thirty-first Convention*, 1960, p. 9. The motion was ruled out of order.
3. *Proceedings of the Thirtieth Convention*, 1954, pp. 332–333.
4. *Proceedings of the Thirty-first Convention*, 1960, p. 9.
5. *Proceedings of the Twenty-ninth Convention*, 1950, p. 83.

CHAPTER 8

1. The list of officers and occupations of the 1960 delegates is from *Proceedings of the Thirty-first Convention*, 1960, p. 111. The miscellaneous occupations are from *Proceedings of the Thirtieth Convention*, 1954, p. 106, and *Proceedings of the Twenty-ninth Convention*, 1950, p. 335.
2. *Proceedings of the Thirty-first Convention*, 1960, p. 529.
3. For the list of committee members, see *ibid.*, pp. 18–21. The voting machine committee appears on p. 220. The main list of guards is given on pp. 235–237, with additional names on pp. 561, 631, and 650–651. Duplication in the lists of guards has been eliminated.
4. *Ibid.*, pp. 9, 247, 251.
5. *Proceedings of the Thirtieth Convention*, 1954, p. 11.
6. The leaflet is reproduced in Edens, *Enemies of Bill Lee and Foes of the Trainmen's Brotherhood* (Waco, Texas: Kelley-Bone Ptg. Co., no date), pp. 27–32.
7. Titler, *Our Fight for Democracy*, foreword and p. 1 (italics in original).
8. *Proceedings of the Thirtieth Convention*, 1954, pp. 609–613.
9. *Proceedings of the Thirty-first Convention*, 1960, p. 5.
10. *Proceedings of the Committee of the Whole, Thirty-first Convention*, 1960, p. 7.
11. *Ibid.*, pp. 41–47.
12. *Proceedings of the Thirty-first Convention*, 1960, pp. 197, 201.
13. *Proceedings of the Committee of the Whole, Thirty-first Convention*, 1960, pp. 14–18.
14. *Ibid.*, pp. 119–120.
15. *Ibid.*, pp. 107–110.
16. Two years later the proposal was made that Kennedy, along with the entire Board of Directors, remain in office until the expiration of their full terms or until the following convention was held. The reasons as-

signed were the impact of the expected report of the Presidential Commission on work rules and employment in the industry, and the need for experienced leadership to deal with commuter problems of passenger roads. The proposal was viewed by the administration group as an effort by Weil supporters to block Luna's automatic succession to the presidency, thereby giving Weil a better opportunity to win election to that post at the next convention.

17. *Proceedings of the Thirty-first Convention,* 1960, pp. 664–671, 687–688.
18. *Ibid.,* pp. 684–685.

CHAPTER **9**

1. The 460 Club functioned openly in the post-convention period, without any effort to discipline its leaders for their activities in its behalf. However, John McGinness, president of the club, was removed from the presidency of Lodge 225 in December, 1961, for putting to a lodge vote a motion to change the dues structure without advance notice as required by the union's constitution and the Labor-Management Reporting and Disclosure Act. The motion, without changing lodge monthly dues, reduced the assessment for handling grievances by sixty cents, while increasing the sum for regular operating expenses by a like amount. At the hearing McGinness was also found guilty of refusing to accept charges against himself at a meeting of his lodge, and of adjourning the meeting, which had become quite disorderly, and leaving it without following proper closing procedures. Besides removing him from office, Kennedy barred him indefinitely from representing the union in any capacity. McGinness thereupon filed an appeal to the next convention.
2. *Report of the Board of Directors, 1956,* pp. 90–91.

Index